Beyond Countertransference

COMMENTARY

"A beautiful book. *Beyond Countertransference* demonstrates the brave self inquiry clinicians often preach but somehow seldom practice. Natterson's consistent struggle against authoritarian reductionism and scientistic certainty, his telling explorations of his countertransferences and of other aspects of his subjectivity, and his clear observations regarding the role of reciprocal subjectivities in the psychotherapeutic encounter should inform and inspire clinicians of many disciplines and many persuasions. Beyond that, *Beyond Countertransference* is a moving study in and of creativity."

—M. Robert Gardner, M.D.

"This iconoclastic book challenges all previous psychoanalytic assumptions about the mode of action of psychological treatment. Readers of every persuasion will be stimulated to rethink their favored theories of technique and therapeutic change. Natterson's contributions should lead to a fruitful controversy for some time to come."

—John Gedo, M.D.

"This is not a simple book in which an experienced analyst 'tells all' about himself. It offers a stimulus to therapists to understand how their subjectivity (not their countertransference) shapes the profound interpersonal experience of psychoanalytic therapy. In my opinion, Dr. Natterson's formulations have implications for theory and practice that may well become a milestone in psychoanalytic theory."

—Saul Brown, M.D.

Beyond Countertransference

The Therapist's Subjectivity in the Therapeutic Process

JOSEPH NATTERSON, M.D.

JASON ARONSON INC.
NORTHVALE, NEW JERSEY
LONDON

Library of Congress Cataloging-in-Publication Data

Natterson, Joseph M., 1923–
    Beyond countertransference : the therapist's subjectivity in the therapeutic process /
Joseph M. Natterson.
        p.   cm.
    Includes bibliographical references and index.
    ISBN 0-87668-558-0
    1. Psychotherapy.   2. Subjectivity.   3. Psychoanalytic
interpretation.   4. Psychotherapist and patient.   I. Title.
    [DNLM: 1. Professional-Patient Relations.   2. Psychoanalytic
Interpretation.   3. Psychoanalytic Therapy.   WM 460.6 N282t]
RC489.S83N38   1991
616.89'14—dc20
DNLM/DLC
for Library of Congress   90-14542

Manufactured in the United States of America. Jason Aronson Inc. offers books and cassettes. For information and catalog write to Jason Aronson Inc., 230 Livingston Street, Northvale, New Jersey 07647.

Contents

Preface

This book argues that the therapist's subjectivity is an indispensable component of the therapeutic process. This focus arises from clinical experience, and the presentation abounds in clinical examples. It is my conviction that previous approaches to this matter have been inadequate or misleading. Therefore, I also review traditional psychodynamic concepts to show how they have generated confusion and impeded optimal utilization of the therapist's subjectivity.

My thesis is that the subjective life of the therapist is coequal to that of the patient in creating the therapeutic transaction. This point is shown in many ways throughout the book, so that it becomes available practically to serious psychotherapists and students.

In order to accomplish this goal, the book's ingredients consist of clinical material from patients, personal data from the therapist, and theoretical discussions. These three elements weave around one another, like a triple helix, throughout the book. Thus the subjective life of the therapist is shown to be integral and inseparable from the verbal and nonverbal behavior of the patient. The theoretical discussion is closely linked to the personal and clinical data, so that its relevance to the living events is consistently evident.

In fact, the book drastically revises certain basic theoretical assumptions regarding the therapeutic process; for instance, the concept of countertransference as the basic explanation of therapists' subjective involvement is refuted. This change enables therapists to appreciate more freely and less guiltily the extent of their subjective participation in every therapeutic moment.

Interpretation traditionally enjoys the highest status as a therapeutic intervention. Therefore, I chose the interpretative process as the focus for demonstrating how the therapist's subjective life enters the scene of the therapy. I show that interpretation and intersubjectivity are indispensable to each other. Furthermore, interpretation, as a powerful intersubjective act and manifestation, becomes much more than a mere technical device of psychotherapy. From this standpoint, we can then see the following: interpretation occurs in nonverbal as well as verbal forms, interpretation reflects and shapes the self, and interpretation exists in rich dialogical relation to dreams. Clinical case excerpts provide convincing background material. The intersubjective origins, manifestations, and correlations of interpretation are demonstrated by these instances of profound patient–therapist reciprocity.

In addition to the numerous clinical illustrations throughout the book, there is also a substantial chapter on the clinical categories of interpretation, with suitable case reports—ample enough to make the point fully, but sufficiently brief to maintain the interest of the reader.

Another important component of the book consists of explicit guidelines enabling the therapist to

1. achieve optimal self scrutiny

2. utilize patients' criticism and hostility to achieve enriched intersubjective insight

3. choose fluently between verbal and nonverbal responses

4. manage various other "technical" challenges facing the therapist.

The traditional misunderstanding and neglect of the therapist's subjectivity has seriously diminished the power and refinement of much therapeutic work. This book sets forth the principles and methods necessary for the achievement of a sophisticated, intersubjectively informed psychotherapy.

This work challenges the current tendency to subsume intersubjectivity exclusively to the school of therapy called self psychology. Instead, the intersubjective experience properly constitutes the basic precondition for any theoretical explanation of psychotherapy, whether it is Freudian, self psychological, interpersonal, or other.

The book is a handbook for both the practitioner and the student who wishes for a major enhancement of his or her therapeutic understanding and power.

Acknowledgment

The spirit of this book dwells in the powerful human relationships it recounts. The persons who helped create these intimate events are therefore intrinsic to the book, even as it goes beyond narrative into concept and method. Although I alone am responsible for the book and its contents, its essence belongs to the people who, along with me, inhabit the following pages.

For obvious reasons, I cannot identify those persons who provided the basis for this project, so I have decided to forego individual acknowledgments. To all the patients, students, colleagues, family, and friends who helped and encouraged me, my most profound thanks for all you have done. You know who you are. I know who you are. We will remember!

1

THE AUTHOR'S VOICE

Several wise friends have urged me to begin this project with a personal statement. After all, they say, as though in unison, the book *is* all about your subjectivity, and therefore you must analyze the book according to the principles you assert.

Where, in you, did this work arise? How did it develop? What does it really mean to you? You must not separate yourself from the book, as at times you seem to do in some of the more theoretical portions. If your style sometimes becomes stiff and cumbersome, always return to your own self. You say an analysis is incomplete without the analyst's self. Well, so is this book incomplete without the author's self. Take the risk. Do it!

Ignorance and fear produce my reluctance. I do not know what to say, and I am fearful of knowing. The result is a characteristic state of indecisiveness not only about expressing an opinion, but more basically in claiming that an opinion that I hold at the moment is a fact. Having made this confession, however, I have reduced and contained my shame over ignorance and fear, and feel freer now to proceed.

The following impressions will lack balance and completeness; they express my subjective experience at the time of writing. I wrote with no intention of producing an accurate chronicle. As I reread my comments, I realize how unfair they are to my father, my mother, my siblings—and to myself. However, aside from adding a little stain to some already tarnished memories, I don't perceive that any damage is done.

My psychological being depends almost totally upon contact with and relation to other people. Without these relationships, I have never known who or what I am or anything about the world around me. This results in a conviction that I lack a human existence except through my relationships. I cannot precisely describe how I might feel, stripped of human contact, but nevertheless the sense of the indispensability of such contacts is very powerful.

This realization had not been firmly conscious for me prior to the construction of this book. Many fragmentary conscious experiences should have brought it to me, but I suppose the implications were so anxiety-provoking that I managed to skirt them.

A companion experience of my consciousness has been an ever-present tendency to feel inadequate, ill informed, and prone to grievous error. These worries over inadequacy or erring abate when a relationship becomes active and reassuring, either through meeting my dependency needs or through the experience of being loved. Of course, the two are often indistinguishable.

I realize that the sense of not existing and the feelings of inadequacy may well be expressions of the same fundamental neurotic characteristics. However, here I am less concerned about whether these traits are normal or neurotic than I am about their likely role in producing the conclusions and recommendations I have set forth in this book. It is second nature for me to be unable to know, and therefore to avoid expressing opinions, including interpretations, without a simultaneous interdependent transaction with another person or persons. Perhaps a fringe benefit of my particular neurotic disorder is a heightened sensitivity to certain universal characteristics of the human experience that may be less evident to others who enjoy more inner comfort and confidence.

Looking back from my sixty-fifth year, I am shocked that I have held so few firm opinions about action issues. But how could it be otherwise if all of my beliefs and opinions are ultimately anchored to relationships and in view of the inevitable fluctuations in the intensity and the quality of relationships? Of course, I do have certain constant, sustained characteristics, both attitudinal and behavioral, but my subjective sense of myself all too often excludes these considerations.

Throughout my life, or so my memory tells me, my ideas lacked conviction unless I could obtain corroborative agreement or disagreement from another person or persons. In all experience, I invariably arrive quickly at the edge of the world of meaning and teeter anxiously as I peer into the dark abyss of ignorance and unknowing. A part of me is convinced that my ideas or even the thoughts of others can never bring much light to this endless zone of darkness, although there is also an undercurrent of incorrigible hopefulness and curiosity. I can enjoy only moments of confidence, certitude, belief, and an attendant feeling of joy. A favorite metaphor of mine is that life consists of moving through a fog. We reach occasional clearings where lucidity and understanding prevail. Soon thereafter, the fog once again envelops us, and we move on in search of another brief moment or zone of clarity.

What does this have to do with intersubjectivity and, more pointedly, my own subjectivity? Simply, my amorphous, slippery consciousness has left me no choice; I am compelled to turn to others. He, she, they, will make sense of this or that, of the world, will give me meaning, will show me the right path to follow. Despite this hope, however, my skepticism eventually triumphs and destroys the delightful interlude of knowing. I then repudiate the enlightenment and its provider, and I go on and on, repeating the cycle endlessly. In a sense, this is what fills my life. Perhaps the same is true of all people, regardless of the different forms it may take. Is it any wonder that I think the basic principle of human psychology is people influencing people, imposing their respective wills on one another, with each and all deriving any personal sense of being and meaning from that process?

My personal version of the intersubjective experience has undoubtedly been conditioned by the fact that I was the youngest child in a family of seven—a mother, a father, and four older sisters. As I remember the family in childhood and later, we were and are conscientious, interesting, intelligent, suffering, conflicted, and confused people. Everyone else was older and more experienced. I felt surrounded by a mass of experts, unlike me. But I also knew that their human weakness was such that they could not really be wise. They seemed not to understand me and perhaps not themselves or one another. Yet I must emphasize that this impression of their frailties coexisted and an equal opposing sense of their masterful understanding. Both traits somehow made them different from me.

Quite early I resolved that I would avoid the errors of those around me, whose lives were so filled with pain. And how would I do this? By the simple act of remembering all the significant events as they occurred, so that there would be no missing links in the chain of causality. Through this, I would understand myself and be blessed with the capacity not to contribute to error. Perhaps in this way, I could guarantee happiness for myself, or perhaps it was more of an effort to establish a kind of moral superiority. I don't know for how long I attempted to maintain this unrealistic standard, but eventually I became aware that like all other people, I had failed in this grandiose endeavor. I was trapped along with everyone else by repression, conflict, ambivalence, and the other complications that stud all our lives. This effort to avoid fateful error reflected my effort to cope with the intersubjective imperative. Probably, my own difficulties in early relationships alerted me to the hazards of interdependence. In my futile efforts to avoid the pitfalls of interdependence, I was also insulating myself against trusting relationships. From an intersubjective standpoint, I was obstructing the pathway to development of the self. Later, when I realized what I had done, I became more able to appreciate the absolute importance of other people for my own consciousness as a human being and therefore for my development as a person.

One indication of a greater maturity is that I am much more aware of the many ways I am flawed and am much more able to acknowledge these to myself and others. At the same time, I feel more confident and happier with being who I am. I believe further that these developments have coincided with a greater capacity to be close to people, to take from people knowingly, and to acknowledge that my being was inseparable from theirs.

As a child, one of my delusions was a sense of messianic importance that I was necessary for the entire universe, and at the same time another laughable conviction that nothing but me really existed in the universe. I must have felt devoid of any kind of substantial meaning. The achievement of stable, loving relationships was, understandably, a long, hard struggle for me. The issues just described may give some general indication of why this was so. My desperate realization that only through the terrifying prospect of forming relationships could I discover and become myself etched the concept of intersubjectivity deep into my mind long before I could define it consciously.

Midway through high school, I discovered Sigmund

Freud. An uncle who was visiting brought me a copy of *Moses and Monotheism,* and it was a revelation. It confirmed that my doubts about received truth concerning God and the history of the Jews were justified. Freud attempted to subvert conventional beliefs and offered a new and more drastic set of convictions to replace them. I welcomed this because of the iconoclastic pleasure that it provided me, and because it reflected a more genuine effort to discover the truth of our origins and our meanings. However, it seems to me that even at that early time, when I became a sort of Freudian, I soon became skeptical about him and suspected that his subversion was probably also invalid because, after all, how could he know? So, in swift succession, I rejoiced in the arrival of the true knower, Freud, and very quickly began to doubt and question and, at least silently, rebel.

This incorrigible skepticism has persisted. It even applies to this book. At times I am convinced of the validity of the notions I present, while at other times I shudder with a sense of profound humiliation that I have attempted to purvey such superficial nonsense when others who are stronger and more stable disagree with me. So this has been a difficult project, although at times a pleasing one. Above all, its personal, intimate nature has been an ever-present part of my authorial experience. Some of its intimate meaning for me has been its very contradictory quality, that is, in each sentence I have struggled between expressing myself in an informal, very personal, even intimate way, versus an effort to subordinate those inclinations to a more professional, reflective sort of discourse. Perhaps this continuous, fundamental contradiction throughout the writing has created a valuable tension in the book.

I believe this book should have been written from within psychoanalysis a number of years ago. I wish I had done it sooner. My personal struggle toward the production of the book illustrates the basic theme, the indispensable role of the subjective life of the analyst/author in the creation of an analysis/book.

I am attempting to demonstrate that my fantasies and desires can be harmonized productively with the world of people who exist around me. Perhaps I am attempting to prove the point I state in the book: each of us is continuously trying to impose our own view of the universe on the rest of the universe, while also needing to be influenced by others. A relationship invariably is a process of continuous reciprocal influence.

The intersubjective principle becomes real for me through the emotionally powerful experiences in my life. I gain accretions of consciousness especially as a result of periods of great joy or deep pain. The pains seem to teach me more about the intersubjective nature of my relationships than do the joys. I think this is so because of my pervasive guilt. If any unhappiness occurs in a circumstance in which I bear responsibility, I reflexively assume total responsibility. How much better it would be to realize that, yes, I'm no angel, but neither are the involved others.

But I persist in my belief that I was born, therefore I was responsible for my parents' marital unhappiness and their economic burdens. I was the youngest, so I must have been parasitic and debilitating for the others. My childish irritability engendered ambient unpleasantness in the family. My sexuality was dirty and sinful, sullying the noble values of the family and the neighborhood. If on the street a little friend was hurt during our play, it was surely my fault. Conversely, no one but I was responsible for my own injuries and close calls. In childish sex play, I was corrupt, the other was a despoiled innocent. And so it emerged through the epochs of my life. I have always played the role of fugitive cum victim, being pursued by the posse of guilt.

This absurd but compelling scenario takes new and interesting forms as my life journey proceeds. In recent years a misunderstanding with my extended family occurred on the occasion of my eldest sister's death. I took an action that at the time I thought correct. However, it was offensive to most of the family. In reaction, I could not achieve a balanced view of the difficult position we all occupied. Instead, I swung wildly between profound guilt–shame and extreme indignation–outrage, with inevitable disruption of my grief-work. Once more, I repeated my totalistic emotional response, to my great disadvantage.

How much better it all could have been! Unfortunately, no one possessed the knowledge or courage to offer an intersubjective analysis to the frightened boy who attempted to achieve coherence of meaning by organizing experience around unilateral moral responsibility, laced with bitterness, its ugly companion. Optimally, the more experienced family members should have explained that parents have a sexual relationship because they enjoy it and that they accept emotional responsibility for the offspring. Furthermore, children play a crucial and constructive role in a healthy family—they are not burdensome and damaging to the family. Children need to engage in vigorous play and explore the incipience of sexuality—these activities entail risks that must be taken. And so on.

But this could not happen in my family; and no blame need be assigned. None of us could effectively recognize and communicate the basic truth: we were all bound up in one another; the actions and desires—conscious and unconscious—of each of us influenced and were influenced by similar processes in the others. The open and consistent acknowledgment of shared responsibility attenuates harsh moral judgment of oneself or others, and a more supple sense of personal responsibility arises.

I learned well that patients' furious, urgent protests about me—or others—are thinly disguised pleas that I understand the intersubjective nature of the painful situation. In so many words, the patient is really saying: I know I made a mistake, I was vaguely aware that I needed to hurt someone, but I was not the only tactless, hostile, or neglectful player. I do not deserve the wholesale reproach I am visiting upon myself. Help me to stop it. If, as therapist, I can find some way to share the person's culpability, that person can then assume constructive responsibility for his or her motives and actions—and their consequences.

It is very easy to render narrow interpretations of hostile, unconscious motives of the other person. Anyone who has ever been on the receiving end of interpretations that do not in some way include the subjective involvement of the interpreter can realize that these are very poor interpretations indeed.

It has always been my practice to avoid categorical assertions of knowledge. I prefer to say, "I think," "I believe," "I suspect," "I wonder" rather than "I know." It has always seemed essential for me to leave some significant space for the other person's possibly different and possibly more valid interpretation of meaning. A genuine appreciation of life's complexity and contradictions inherent in the tentativeness of such a stance always implies the possibility of error in one's own judgment. I am now aware of additional, ignoble, motives.

I was also attempting, unconsciously, to protect my family members from my aggression and from their acknowledgment of their own aggression. In this regard, my attitude and stance has, in the very recent past, ripened fruitfully. I now recognize the extent of my readiness to accept scapegoating as an unacknowledged form of trying to absorb everyone's aggression and to let my own aggression be openly acknowledged, which had a corollary effect of seeming to neutralize the virulence of my own aggression. This, on my part, had been an acceptable if dishonest arrangement. But only for so long as I was essentially supported as a "nice boy" rather than massively repudiated.

I now must alter my fundamental arrangement with

myself and my intimate others. And as part of this "growing up," I attempt to enlarge the insight that we all contribute to the psychological circumstances in which we participate.

The painful occurrences around the death of my sister became an extremely powerful and convincing example for me of the validity of intersubjectivity. This concept, which is invariably applicable to all human circumstances, was exemplified in a very useful way for me through this personal experience. Primarily I could feel and need the recognition of the co-responsibility of all the participants in this drama. And I was able to generalize to a realization that in all human encounters the recognition of such co-responsibility is the enabling event for understanding and for constructive outcome. The acknowledgment and analysis of one's own neurotic input renders one ever so much more able to perceive the counterpart contribution of the others. The reverse is also true—namely, a realization that others are contributing and are able to acknowledge their contribution renders one much more able to acknowledge one's own. In a sense, this is what intersubjectivity as a clinical and theoretical resource is all about.

I am stressing the need, or I should say the inevitability, of analysts bringing their own personal experiences and personal meanings and goals into their participation and understanding of the analytic process. And I believe that the reader of this book should know something more about me, in order that the book not be experienced as some disembodied set of abstract or unrelated ideas. They express me as well as my experience and my generalizations and recommendations.

Either by inner disposition or as a function of experience and habit, analysts tend to be isolated, and not to be joiners. We practice a solitary profession, often sitting out of sight of our patients and concentrating upon them and our own ongoing inner experience. In a sense, my early life prepared me for this career. I am the youngest of five children, the only son of economically impoverished and politically radical Russian Jewish immigrants. Being poor, Jewish, and left wing was not a rarity during the 1920s, but being all of these things and living in Appalachia did give an accent to the feeling of being different. I always felt a sense of deprivation and alienation, but at the same time my experiences fostered an empathic capability that, to my guilty regret, I certainly did not always practice.

My father was a sensitive and talented man, but he was deeply troubled in ways that have always been mysterious to me. The terrible economic stress of the late 1920s and 1930s depleted him, and for me, he became a weak and ineffectual father. This provided me with an unsolicited oedipal victory and a strong feminine identification, the latter reinforced by my mother's ambivalent assumption of the role of head of the family. The squelching of my maleness was completed inadvertently by my four older sisters. Fortunately, I possessed enough innate or acquired ego strength to stumble through one awful epoch after another. As I staggered into adulthood, I retained sufficient critical judgment to realize that the world offers a different set of possibilities than those of my childhood and youth.

Two powerful global events helped shape me: the Great Depression and World War II. The first reinforced and augmented my sense of economic and societal marginality and amplified my already existing doubts about the justice and kindness of our society. But ironically, by giving me the opportunity to have a university education, which might otherwise have been very difficult for me, World War II provided personal liberation and developmental stimulation for me. Of course, becoming a physician did not remove the traits I had developed so strongly earlier, and I remained an insecure person, yearning for acceptance and security but not knowing how to achieve it.

So I have always lived subjectively on the edge of society. A life of poverty, being the youngest and hence the

most ignorant and inexperienced, and the feelings about
being an only male child in a family in which the husband
and father was extremely insecure and largely ineffectual in
his role deepened my sense of difference, alienation, and
insecurity. As time passed I became what I am now, an urban,
prosperous Jew living in the midst of similar Jews, though
the inner tentative quality of my life is unabated. Earlier I
regretted that my religion, my politics, my economic class,
and the other serious effects of the constellation in my family
of origin distanced me from society. Now, however, I view
this as more of a strength than a weakness, and I do not wish
to embrace the conventions of a world in which the people
abuse its inhabitants and its environment so terribly. Like
Pangloss, I am wise enough to admit that I cannot change
the world. But I can attempt, in my personal life, to develop
my consciousness and to use my subjectivity as powerfully
as possible in my work, which is intended to be of help to
other individuals.

The preceding comments, while accurate, are also incomplete. They represent more a glimpse, an epitome, of a
subjective paradigm, than a true exposition and explanation.
I have tried to express a process in anguish that began prior
to the dawn of memory and persists, although highly attenuated, to this day. I have learned in this struggle that I am
just a part of the universe and it is a part of me. That is what
the book is about.

2

INTERSUBJECTIVITY IN THE THERAPEUTIC PROCESS

The following clinical vignette exemplifies the intersubjective nature of therapeutic action. It is only one of literally thousands of therapeutic events that could have been chosen to set the stage for this chapter.

An unmarried poet in her middle thirties was in analysis because of anxiety and loneliness. She also had a blood dyscrasia, and she wanted help in developing the better dietary habits that were necessary to maintain her health. After about two years of analysis she had a dream:

It is evening, the light is dim. I am in a shacklike house, in a room with other people. An army is approaching; it is going for the people in the house who are refugees. But I am not a refugee; rather I am there to help the others escape the army.

The youngest of the people is a boy. Yesterday, he walked a long distance to reach the house. He is exhausted and undernourished. I am worried about his ability to make

17

it to the top of the mountain. I feel much anguish over him.

As all this is happening, I am simultaneously going up the mountain. I may be a child rather than an adult. My legs ache, it is a terrible ordeal, I do not know whether I can go on. But my survival depends on my going on. It begins to rain, it is a freezing downpour, I become soaked through with this terrible cold. It is awful, I think I will have to accept death, and I sit down in defeat. But a man talks with me, and he says the right things. Then I am able to go on somewhat further.

The boy is able to reach his destination on the other side of the mountain, where he is safe and secure and warm. The man who helped me is the same person as the boy in the dream. A good feeling arises in me; I will be able to make it to the top of the mountain.

This dream beautifully demonstrates the intersubjective nature of the therapeutic process. The dream also consolidates growing insight and consequent ego change in the dreamer. We both perceived the dream as a major milestone in therapeutic progress.

Her associations were direct and powerfully congruent with mine. She associated to her need to escape from her childhood, her adolescence, and even her adult life prior to her analysis. Her parents were her enemies, as were the others, mostly men, to whom she had entrusted her well-being previous to her analysis. In addition to the lack of intimacy in her life, she suffered a severe eating disorder. By the time of this dream, she had mastered her eating problem and its psychological causes. She knows that the arduous ascent symbolizes her struggle in the analysis. Her battle is not entirely over, but she can see safety and happiness on the other side of the mountain.

The patient realizes that I am the man who helps her, and the boy symbolizes both of us. She has inferred, confidently and correctly, that my own life difficulties are similar to hers, and that I too have struggled up the mountain of life.

In the earlier phase of the analysis her anxiety was so discouraging that often she could not speak. I therefore frequently spoke for her, accurately expressing in words the thoughts and feelings that she could convey only in nonverbal modes. Through this repeated experience she could perceive my psychological likeness to her, feel love for me, and gradually develop a belief in her own lovability, which had been massively damaged by her exploitive parents. Her mother's role was especially corrosive of the patient's self-definition. The cycle of loving me, being loved by me, and then believing in her lovability recurred until her gains in self-esteem culminated in this dream. She revealed her awareness that she and I are different and yet the same. Fundamentally, the perilous ascent represented her highest achievement: the conviction that she is lovable. Unless she believes this, it is very difficult for her to survive.

This accomplishment unleashed an apparently paradoxical reaction. She began experiencing hatred toward me for the first time in the analysis. Although she maintained her newly won feeling of being lovable and continued to avoid abusing herself with food, she became convinced that I did not really care deeply about her and that I could sacrifice her interests for mine or others'. This painful reaction constituted the emergence and shared experience of a deep negative mother transference of great transformational significance for the analysis.

I responded with a hurt and self-protective feeling. This reaction helped me to become even more clearly aware than previously that I have always been motivated by fantasies of rescuing my mother and eldest sister from their realistic misfortunes and also from my own aggression. Thus the patient was, from my standpoint, disproving my lovingness and my lovability.

This Gordian knot of love, hate, guilt, and fear that bould us together eventually dissolved rather than being severed. She and I communicatively achieved a more intense oneness and fusion, and at the same time we each individuated and differentiated from one another more completely. This was the same theme as in the dream: she was herself, I was the man, and we were both the boy.

The second intersubjective illustration concerns a divorced female Eurasian artist. She had been in therapy with me for several years. The earlier period of the treatment had centered on her chronic, unresolved grief reaction to the murder of her only child, a daughter, some seventeen years earlier. Recently, she had become much freer of this terrible encumbrance.

The restoration of her well-being became associated with more focused career activity and a determination to improve her unsatisfactory financial position. She also resolved to seek and find a man with whom she could achieve a fulfilling involvement.

In addition to a father–daughter polarization of our relationship that resulted from our generational and gender differences, there was also a quality of contrasting expertise. It was as though I instructed her in the relevant aspects of psychoanalysis, while she introduced me to their counterparts in the Buddhist praxis.

One afternoon she was unable to attend her session, so we talked on the telephone. She informed me that she would soon undertake extensive travel serially with three different men. Two men wished to marry her, but she found them unsuitable. The third man, married and powerful, was the one with whom she was eager to travel. And she stated, "I don't care if he thinks I'm a courtesan."

I responded by saying that if he really regarded her as a courtesan, he was not appropriately respectful of her. She immediately bristled; she felt criticized and devalued by me. I quickly apologized. I reminded her that she, not I, had introduced the term, and I read her Webster's dictionary definition of the word, which has a definite devaluing quality. None of this resolved our acute, painful impasse.

While the patient was on her trip, I reflected extensively on how I might have unconsciously introduced some perturbing attitude of my own into the process. I was certain that I had contributed to the problem because of my nagging feelings of guilt and ineptitude. My associations became powerful and convincing. I began thinking of myself in prepuberty. My two attractive, dark-haired older sisters were engaged in passionate romances, each with a man somewhat older, non-Jewish, and in the eyes of my family, representative of the oppressive, anti-Semitic establishment. I perceived that my mother was furious about these relationships. I recalled my reaction as quite split, including both fascination with these powerful men and also indignation over what I regarded as my sisters' disloyal, shameless behavior. I am sure it is unnecessary for me to mention that the subtext of this split reaction was my complicated erotic and dependent emotions toward my various siblings and my parents. The patient had the momentary misfortune to be in the path of these ruthless sentiments.

When the patient returned to therapy, I insisted that we resume our discussion of the unpleasant encounter, and I acknowledged that her remarks converged with a dormant memory of mine and its thunderous underlying passions. She responded by telling me that she too had done some important work. She realized that she had never told me that her Caucasian mother had been a taxi dancer who had met and married the patient's father, who belonged to a prominent family, in the course of her professional activity. The patient was now becoming more aware that her chronic angry, repudiating attitudes to her mother reflected her shame over her own unconscious identification with the debased, devalued mother.

The painful incident with me had been a crucial event in the achievement of experiential mastery over this previously unacknowledged problem. Our shared capacity to encounter and explore the intersubjective aspects of this issue lent therapeutic intensity to the process, to our mutual benefit.

This incident illustrates dramatically the principle that the subjective experiences of *both* patient and therapist are indispensable ingredients of the therapeutic phenomenon.

This book is about intersubjectivity. It is also a study of interpretation, which, as the definitive intervention by the therapist, carries the encoded subjective involvement of the therapist in his or her most proximate contact with the subjective experience of the patient.

I will demonstrate the origins and unfolding of the intersubjective process both theoretically and clinically. Because this important part of therapeutic action can be captured and coherently presented, its clinical application can be taught; this constitutes another basic part of this book.

Psychodynamic psychotherapists have always implicitly recognized the essential intersubjective elements in the therapeutic process. But this awareness has been clouded by the efforts of traditional theorists to squeeze psychoanalytic therapy into the Procrustean bed of nineteenth-century science. Freud accorded importance to the role of the analyst's subjective experience in the analytic process, but he was of two minds on the subject: either he viewed the analyst's unconscious contribution as negative, that is, countertransference, or he viewed it as positive, that is, a necessary component of the analytic instrument. He never successfully reconciled these opposing viewpoints.

Also, Freud believed that instinctual drives motivate our psychological lives, a belief that naturally led to an intrapsychic theory of personality development and of the origins of neurosis. This in turn inexorably caused Freud to undervalue seriously the significance of the interpersonal factors in both the production of neurosis and the treatment process. His basic theory, therefore, did not permit him to ascribe to intersubjective factors their full significance either early in life or in the later patient–analyst relationship.

Interpretation provides the optimal resource for understanding the intersubjective basis of the therapeutic process, which is why this book focuses on the interpretive process. Two fundamental emphases of traditional psychodynamic thinking must be reduced for an appropriate accommodation to a new understanding of intersubjective factors: (1) the insistence upon an instinctually derived theory of the origin and cure of neurosis that leads naturally to a primarily intrapsychic orientation needs to be drastically deemphasized in favor of intersubjective, interpersonal factors, and (2) the portmanteau concept of countertransference that derives from the intrapsychic orientation also needs to be subordinated to the concept of intersubjectivity. Countertransference remains a most useful concept, but it should not be employed to explain all the subjective reactions of the therapist.

Such theoretical changes will permit the rediscovery of the lost continent of psychodynamic thinking, that is, the therapist's subjectivity, which plays a rich, complex, subtle, and largely unacknowledged role in the therapeutic process. This change, combined with the recent enlarged interest in the self of the patient—in the subjective life of the patient—leads to an exuberant eruption of intersubjective understanding. All this will result in a surge of therapeutic power due to a more balanced appreciation of the various forces at work in psychotherapy. The therapist's subjectivity and the consequent intersubjective events will no longer be neglected.

EARLY AND LATER CONTRIBUTIONS

Here is the voice of Ferenczi (1988) as recorded in his clinical diary in 1932:

> One could almost say that the more weaknesses an analyst has, which lead to greater or lesser mistakes and errors but which are then uncovered and treated in the course of mutual analysis, the more likely the analysis is to rest on profound and realistic foundations. [p. 15]

> Certain phases of mutual analysis represent the complete renunciation of all compulsion and of all authority on both sides: they give the impression of two equally terrified children who compare their experiences, and because of their

common fate understand each other completely and instinc-
tively try to comfort each other. Awareness of this shared
fate allows the partner to appear as completely harmless,
therefore as someone whom one can trust with confidence.
[p. 56]

I do not know of any analyst whose analysis I could declare
theoretically, as concluded (least of all my own). Thus we
have, in every single analysis, quite enough to learn about
ourselves. [p. 194]

Patients *feel* the hypocritical element in the analyst's behavior;
they detect it from hundreds of tiny signs. [p. 200]

These considerations provided the conceptual justification for Ferenczi's extremely controversial method of "mutual analysis," by which Ferenczi meant that from time to
time the analyst and analysand would actually reverse roles.
He might have avoided this egregious recommendation had
the concept of intersubjectivity been available. Of greater
importance here than his technical modification was his implicit recognition of the continuous and crucial intersubjective process in every psychoanalytic therapy, as in every
human encounter.

Alexander (1946), another controversial psychoanalytic
innovator, provided a further contribution to the understanding of the intersubjective grounding of psychodynamic psychotherapy. He developed the concept of the "corrective
emotional experience," which requires that cure be understood to arise from a specific and different kind of emotional
relationship of therapist to patient. Alexander's term, unlike
Ferenczi's, hints at a devaluing of interpretation and insight
in favor of noncognitive experiential factors. But actually,
Alexander's approach was a unified one, in which insight,
achieved through interpretation, constitutes an integral part
of the experiential. His belief in a specific curative interplay
of the personalities of the two parties presaged the intersubjective position.

Winnicott (1958, 1965) was deeply influenced by Freud-ian, Kleinian, and object relations theories, and his origin-ality emerged in a profoundly psychoanalytic context. His construct, the "holding environment," simultaneously in-corporates the historical origins in the intersubjective re-lationship of mother and child, the similar relationship of analyst and patient, and the interpretive essence of the words and actions of both mother and analyst. His constructs have been powerfully influential in the development of contem-porary psychoanalysis and psychodynamic psychotherapy.

Winnicott (1986) says: "If a mother has eight children, there are eight mothers. This is not simply because of the fact that the mother was different in her attitudes to each of the eight. If she could have been the same with each . . . each child would have had his or her own mother seen through individual eyes" (p. 40). In his discussion of "care-cure" (pp. 112–120) he indicates again that this principle of uniqueness also applies to each psychoanalytic relationship.

Another significant precursor of present developments was the concept of *responsive action,* which Grotjahn and I (1965) introduced. We defined responsive action as the ther-apist's genuine and spontaneous reaction to the patient's basic unconscious needs. We recognized the importance of the therapist's technical skill, yet we ascribed a unique signifi-cance to the therapist's responsive action as an essential part of every therapeutic experience.

In the same tradition of elucidating subtle factors in the psychotherapeutic process, Gedo (1981) develops a theory of noninterpretive interventions. He classifies these according to the regressive or progressive condition of the patient's psychological function. These ideas of Gedo will be discussed further in the chapter on guidelines for optimal therapist self-scrutiny. At this point Gedo's ideas about the analyst's sub-jectivity are more pertinent. He states: "Whenever he [the analyst] becomes aware of his own subjective response to the analysand's associative material through introspection, that affective state must be regarded as a highly significant element of the overall pattern to be understood, as Gardner [1983] has recently shown in convincing detail" (p. 164).

Gedo (1981) also states: "In order to assess the significant meanings of another person's communications, the analyst cannot rely on objective criteria, he is forced to screen this material through his own hierarchy of goals and values. Hence the core of the analytic enterprise consists of the analyst's ongoing self-inquiry" (p. 373). Gedo cites the work of Gardner (1983) as a convincing demonstration of these points. Gardner provides a vivid portrait of his own continuous subjective experiences in the course of his analytic work, and he shows how indispensable these events are to the analytic process.

Gedo (1981), referring to his and Goldberg's (1973) work, states: "The disparate clinical theories in common psychoanalytic usage should not be regarded as competing conceptualizations but as valid fragments of a larger whole" (p. 256). Gedo points in these citations to the immensity of the task of achieving a systematic clinical theory, and in effect he is endorsing adherence to the principle of ambiguity in conceptualizing psychoanalysis. This becomes very important as a point of view for detailed understanding of the interplay of the subjective life of the analyst with that of the patient. The only possible systematic position is that the analyst must consistently endeavor to recognize the uniqueness of each such transaction and utilize this recognition in the construction of each and every interpretation.

Peterfreund (1983) declares that psychoanalytic therapy will be either stereotypical or heuristic, the latter being preferable. Theoretical and technical preferences must be subordinated to the genuine therapeutic requirements, which can be recognized only if the therapist is open to the idiosyncratic meanings and needs of the particular patient. It becomes antitherapeutic to rely primarily on general principles in dealing with individual patients.

Peterfreund also states, "In brief, we are never truly 'neutral' observers and interpreters. In every word and comment we implicitly convey something of our own life experience, our standards and beliefs, something of what we feel about the patient as a human being. How could it be otherwise?" (p. 108). Similarly, regarding the analyst's mental activity, he writes: "The terms *evenly hovering attention* or *evenly suspended attention* (Freud 1912) are useful descriptive expressions, but they tell us little about the underlying process. I believe that these terms can be said to refer to an experience resulting from very rapid information retrieval and highly complex processing, including the rapid testing of many hypotheses. The analyst is very active in his supposedly 'passive' listening state; but it is a special kind of activity" (p. 109). While Peterfreund does not discuss intersubjectivity, his recognition of the complexity and distinctiveness of each therapist's involvement in the treatment clearly moves our understanding of the therapeutic process further toward an interactive intersubjective basis.

Much recent work in psychoanalytic therapy indirectly supports the need for greater attention to the therapist's subjectivity. An example of this genre of investigation is the work of Bach (1985). He discusses special requirements in the treatment of narcissistic patients. His illustrations reveal a marvelously subtle and textured quality to the therapist's attitude to intervention. Such attunement would require a profound and sustained immersion by the therapist in his or her own subjectivity.

Pine (1985) provides further evidence of the remarkable complexity and obscurity of psychoanalytic processes. Pine demonstrates this by an integration of current knowledge of development and the various influential clinical theories. He proposes that the four major concepts applying to neurosogenesis and treatment are all useful theoretical emphases at different points during therapy. These four models are drive/conflict, object relations, ego psychology, and self psychology. Pine's eclecticism further diminishes the dominance of instinct/drive theory and the related notion of the intrapsychic origin and cure of neurosis.

The preceding authors' contributions are in various ways quite disparate. In common, however, they lead us to a clearer awareness of the subjective contribution of the therapist to the therapeutic process.

THEORETICAL BASE OF THERAPIST'S SUBJECTIVE ROLE

All human two-person transactions share fundamental meaning: each party attempts to influence the other with his or her view of the universe to persuade the other of the rightness of his or her view. This basic premise enables us to realize that the value-neutral therapist is a fictive assumption and that this basic power orientation of dyadic relationships makes it natural for moral influences invariably to be significant components of therapists' activity.

In the therapeutic process a creative flux develops from the interaction of the basic beliefs of patient and therapist. These beliefs are inseparable from the fantasies and yearnings of the two persons. If we assume that every interpretation is a statement of meaning about the nature of the universe and all its components—including the subjective life of the interpreter—then it becomes feasible that each interpretation is in part a statement of values and is thus ultimately a moral communication, since moral judgments are basically expressions of a person's beliefs about the nature of the universe. Logically, these beliefs become guiding principles for the person's attitudes and actions. Therapy then results in continuous transformation of these convictions and of their holders; it always has moral meaning.

The work of Weiss and Sampson (1986) makes a related point about the psychoanalytic process. They designate the analysand's "unconscious belief"—usually a deleterious and disruptive one—as being beneficially revised by the analyst's interventions. The analyst enables the analysand to achieve a different and more benign belief so that under favorable conditions, the analysis is able to change the patient's unconscious view of the world. I believe that Weiss and Sampson are basically suggesting that the analyst provides a different belief about the patient and the patient's world from the one learned from parents. Furthermore, this principle applies not only to psychoanalysis, but to all psychotherapy.

In a psychotherapeutic encounter, as in all human dyadic impingements, each person influences the other, no matter how obscure this process may be. Both parties are coequal contributors. Their respective fantasies and desires, values and goals, are engaged in continuous struggle, through which both persons are continuously changing. *This intersubjective experience should be regarded as the basic precondition for any theoretical understanding of psychotherapeutic processes.*

The following clinical excerpt illustrates the reciprocity inherent in the therapeutic process:

> A middle-aged man who is a student of foreign religious and moral influences on Meso-American culture, and who is himself of Japanese ancestry, had been in analysis for several years. He had begun treatment because of a long-standing marital incompatibility and chronic depression with deep feelings of culpability in life.
>
> A strong current of warmth pervaded our first meeting, and these feelings have underlain our relationship throughout the course of therapy. This does not mean that negative tensions have not arisen between us, but such periods have always been subordinated to an overarching trust and affection and have thereby become important contributors to therapeutic progress.
>
> Shortly after beginning treatment, he and his wife sep-

arated. This arrangement continued for over two years, during which time the patient worked very effectively on his strong feelings of guilt and shame, learning about their roots in early life and discovering their manifestations in his transference to me. Partly as a result of these changes, he and his wife restored their loving relationship and have reestablished a life together. He then reported the following dream:

> There is a nuclear disaster. The survivors rush to the beach to escape radiation. The dreamer reaches the beach and finds me there. Someone is speaking, we both listen in order to determine our next step in this crisis. We make a full circle of the beach, and it becomes the island on which he had been born and reared. We make the same loop back to where we began, and we discover there is no place to sleep because all possible resting places are occupied by other refugees. Many of these strangers are in shock. Still worse, the area has some of the ambience of an extermination camp. Are we going to die? Profound gloom is all-pervasive. Then it all changes. A life-giving force now prevails. The dreamer and I clasp hands. That is the moment at which the tender touch pushes back the gloom—affirming the power of the human touch.

His first associations were fears for the preservation of the planet, our species, and a culture worth calling human. He then talked about how helpful my noncoercive, accepting attitude has been in his effort to resolve his problems with his wife. He added that he is also pleased that now, after weeks of difficulty, he has overcome an acute writing block. He is completing an important and controversial paper that he will soon present to an international meeting of scholars. His conscious emotional pain in this session centered on a telephone conversation with his wife shortly before his appointment. He felt hurt by her vagueness, and he suspected that she maintained a lingering interest in another man and that, more disturbing, she was reluctant to discuss the matter with him. The distance between them grew as the conversation proceeded, and it ended quite frostily. The session concluded with the patient immersed in these feelings of discouragement.

Two days later he returned, enthusiastic about the dream and its meaning and about his life. He now felt convinced that basically the dream portrayed the human power of transformation. The love he has always felt to and from me has enabled him to face the complexities of his negative feelings about his wife. Through our careful work he has transformed his debilitating bitterness toward her into an overarching love. Our affirming handshake in the dream was the turning point from despair to hope and joy.

He stated that this most recent episode of suspicion toward his wife led him to the realization that it was also an important expression of helpless frustration over his father's inability ever to engage anyone in genuine and satisfying conversation. The patient noted that, in contrast, he has always been understanding and conciliatory to a fault, like his mother. By discovering in me a fathering person who will talk seriously and respectfully with him, he has become firmer in controversial relationships and no longer projects the worst parts of these negative father feelings on to his wife.

I now became acutely aware that in meeting his needs for a loving paternal response, I was gratifying an immense, similar neediness in myself. His frighteningly picaresque father was quite unlike my father, but the patient and I nevertheless shared a common deficit of effective fathering in childhood. This commonality was a powerful shaping factor for the entire therapy.

This experience of reciprocal fathering and being fathered in the analysis created the powerful intersubjective field for the patient and me. I could also feel a painful admixture of frustrated needs, futile anger, guilt over my discontents, and feeling of loss of strength. I inferred the presence of similar feelings in the patient. I could then employ all this as the mediating force to achieve the following interpretation.

I interpreted his writing block as being linked to the broken finger of his writing hand. (The mishap had occurred recently as he was clumsily retrieving writing materials for the paper he was writing.) I further proposed that their common meaning was the enactment of masochistic inhibition due to guilt toward the infuriatingly frustrating father. I also noted that the handclasp of the dream symbolized his ability to transcend his chronic father problem, that is, the hope and faith in a father that had been accumulating during the analysis achieved culminating, transforming expression in the loving touch of our hands.

We always shook hands at the end of each session, on the patient's original initiative. Then, because of his broken finger, we had to modify our handshake. As this session ended, I did not feel the usual need to participate in the ritual handshake, nor apparently did he. I always enjoyed that moment in the experience of parting, but this time it seemed redundant. We did not shake hands.

Although our cultural, familial, religious, and professional backgrounds are vastly different, he and I have consistently been empathically resonant. My own consciousness of the important principles governing the human condition has grown considerably through our relationship, and I have been undergoing a transformation akin, but subordinate, to his. Because of the patient's exceptional capacity to trace intersubjective processes from the broadest reaches of global politics to the deepest inner privacy of the dream, this auspicious incident of personal and interpersonal transformation seems especially pertinent to a discussion of the intersubjective foundation of interpretive psychotherapy.

According to Habermas (1981), as reported in the pertinent summary by McCarthy (1981), "individuation processes are simultaneously socialization processes, (and conversely), . . motivations and repertoires of behavior are symbolically restructured in the course of identity formation

. . . individual intentions and interests, desires and feelings are not essentially private but tied to language and culture and thus inherently susceptible of interpretation, discussion and change" (p. xx). If we translate these ideas of Habermas into the psychotherapeutic idiom, they inform us that intra-psychic processes are not as self-contained as they may initially appear. Furthermore, it becomes necessary to define psychotherapy as an intersubjective dialogue in which each participant is influencing and being influenced by the other.

These ideas about intersubjectivity as the basic process of psychotherapeutic action are reinforced by the work of Bakhtin (1986). According to Clarke and Holquist (1984), Bakhtin believed no isolated acts exist in consciousness, that every thought connects to other thoughts, including the thoughts of others, and that consciousness is always co-consciousness (p. 77). Sartre (1981) offers the felicitous term "universal singularity" to capture the inevitable coexistence of the communal and the uniquely individual in the self. Furthermore, Clarke and Holquist make clear that Bakhtin considered every human utterance to be an ideological construct, and the motivation of behavior to be invariably moral (p. 182). He makes it clear that value-neutral statements simply cannot be.

In fact, Bakhtin (Clarke and Holquist 1984), speaking of the analytic patient, states: "He wants to foist on the doctor his own point of view on the reasons for his illness and the nature of his experiences" (p. 179). Whereas, he further writes, "the doctor . . . aims at enforcing his authority as a doctor, endeavors to wrest confessions from the patient and to compel him to take the 'correct' point of view on his illness and its symptoms" (pp. 179–180). He specifically designates "struggle" between analyst and patient (p. 180).

Bakhtin's important ideas about the nature of self will be discussed in a later section of this book. Here, I want to emphasize that Bakhtin recognizes the fundamental inseparability of consciousness and human relationships, of psychodynamic therapy and intersubjectivity. And Bakhtin averred that dialogue is the process that creates human meaning, in this way directing our attention to the primary importance of the interpretive dialogue in psychoanalysis and psychotherapy. Thus, Bakhtin becomes a basic theorist of clinical approaches to intersubjectivity and interpretation.

Jacobs (1989) has recently shown, in a series of cases, how the special features of the patient's psychological function elicited various countertransference reactions in him that significantly influenced his mode of relating to the patient. In a summary, Jacobs lamented that in these cases it was not possible to proceed "by the book." Instead, he should have indicated that these examples ultimately demonstrate "the book"—as it should be written—rather than deviate from it.

Spence (1987) has shown that many firmly established psychoanalytic assumptions mistaken for basic truths are, in fact, unacknowledged metaphors. Although Spence appreciates the inevitability and desirability of metaphorical thinking, he also demonstrates that unrecognized metaphors can lead to premature, simplistic, and otherwise false conclusions about the nature of the therapeutic process.

Spence severely criticizes the notions of therapist neutrality and of the therapist's evenly suspended, hovering attention. He writes: ". . . we very likely never hear what the patient is saying in a form that is untouched by our own private accompaniment, and that subjective coloring is a necessary part of understanding" (p. 44). He further insists that in current usage, empathy has a reified and simplistic meaning, as though it were just "another kind of instrument" (p. 44), not the complex interactive phenomenon it in fact is.

Spence relentlessly pursues the complexities of the therapeutic transaction: "The more we feel we truly understand the text or patient and the more it becomes part of our world view, the more likely it will happen that significant mis-understanding is taking place and that what might be called our context of discovery is significantly different from the author's or patient's context of creation" (p. 49). Here Spence is suggesting that the optimal therapist is not unprejudiced; rather he recognizes his inevitable distorting tendencies and their results. One of the results obviously is a flawed inter-pretation. As I discuss later, the therapist should realize not only that every interpretation is significantly flawed, but also that the flaw itself can be a valuable contribution to the therapeutic process.

Spence's work points to an intersubjectively based un-derstanding of psychotherapy that disposes of many shib-boleths that have masqueraded as eternal verities. He insists upon a genuine dialogue between patient and therapist to achieve an "uncompelled consensus" (Habermas 1981), which in our field is the closest possible approximation of objective truth.

Leavy (1980) nicely describes the analyst's subjective involvement in the interpretive process as follows: "[T]he analyst as person, the interpreter to others, is also the inter-preter to himself. He listens and speaks from a world in which he alone is native, even though it is a world also shared with others. It is from this world, this life, this history, that he joins in an exploration of another world, life, history" (p. 68).

My axial theme is the exploration of the powerful and subtle intersubjective factors in the interpretive process and product. These are the same phenomena to which Jacobs refers. Through this understanding, new methodological and technical resources become available to the therapist, with consequent enrichment of the therapeutic experience. As we travel and learn on the king's highway of interpretation, we reach the previously unclaimed territory of the analyst's sub-jectivity, and thereby complete the puzzle that is the inter-subjective reality of psychodynamic psychotherapy.

3

THE TWO STAGES OF INTERPRETATION

In developing an interpretation, the therapist has to choose between generalizing or individualizing—in other words, between whether to emphasize psychological principles or to focus on the patient's immediate experience.

THEORY OF THE TWO STAGES

The dilemma becomes tolerable and even helpful to the therapist if the generalizing activity is undertaken with a sustained awareness of the idiosyncratic nature of each interpretation. Therapists do improve with experience, and the struggle to cope with these choices enlarges the therapist's capacity to make one or another kind of interpretation. But this valuable learned skill, which is a function of the generalizing tendency, becomes a hazard if the therapist forgets the countervailing need to individualize. In practice, the generalized aspect should be passed through the individual experience and couched in language arising from the latter. For example, an interpretation intended to highlight a defense mechanism will be expressed in terms of a very personal issue in the patient's life.

Two contradictory tendencies have to be recognized. The more unique, idiosyncratic, and personalized an interpretation, the more likely it is to be accurate and effective. This fact seems to commend an ambiguous, even anarchic theoretical stance vis-à-vis interpretation. Yet it is also possible to describe similarities that exist among "good" interpretations, or among "bad" ones, so that good and bad interpretations can be distinguished from one another and classified, enabling beginners to learn general characteristics and thus build up a solid base for individualized interpretations.

It should be noted emphatically that the possibility of classification emerges from a clinical matrix in which the therapist should first strive to understand the ambiguous and unique meaning of the interpretation. Only secondarily should the therapist attempt to perceive similarities to other interpretations, which then permit categorization or classification of interpretation. And the interpretation should always be presented to the patient in terms of the patient's life.

It is unwise for a therapist to lean too heavily on the class of interpretation that is being formulated. This bias will obscure rather than clarify the basic intimate elements, thereby causing the therapist to employ *pars pro toto* reasoning to understand why he or she made the interpretation. Conveniently, but mistakenly, the therapist then comes to regard the more obvious part of the truth as the sole basis for the interpretation, and a false understanding is created. Such an oversight may not interfere with a successful therapeutic outcome, but it will obscure crucial factors in the therapeutic action. Attention may be diverted from the most fundamental factors in the production of interpretation: the interplay of the fantasies of the patient and the therapist. Loewald (1960) makes a similar point when he avers that ". . . 'classical' analysis with 'classical' cases easily leave unrecognized essential elements of the analytic process . . ." (p. 231). He too is addressing the complex events occurring between analysand and analyst.

Kohut (1977) asserts that psychoanalytic understanding arises from an *empathic–introspective* stance, which permits *vicarious introspection,* leading to *experience-near* participation. This sequence of events produces the condition called *empathy.* But what preconditions account for the process he describes? Certainly something more elemental than a conscious decision by the analyst to be empathically introspective. More significant is Kohut's emphasis on the therapist's utilization of the countertransference, which contains the seeds of a valid theory of therapeutic action, a sound explanation of empathy, and a complete understanding of interpretation in psychotherapy. While Kohut's work is a major step toward defining the essentials of interpretation, it remains incomplete, especially insofar as it stresses the self–self object aspect of the patient–therapist relationship. Altman (1989) suggests that this defines the analyst as a developmentally necessary *function,* rather than a *person,* and therefore seems to undervalue the reciprocal aspects of the process of therapy.

Stolorow and Atwood (1979) emphasize that the therapist's idiosyncratic life view is reflected in his or her theory and practice of psychotherapy, and they view therapeutic action as occurring in an intersubjective field. Their concepts have helped establish the basis for the careful elucidation of the powerful, reciprocally influential, and mutative transactions between patient and psychotherapist. This view of the psychotherapeutic process leads to a reconsideration of how interpretations arise and of the ways in which they are constituted.

Loewald (1960), Arlow (1979), and Jacobs (1985) argue that interpretations occur in two identifiably distinct but absolutely dependent and necessary stages. The first is the passionate event between patient and therapist that provides the power and the meaning of the interpretation, and the second is the formal construction of the interpretation by the therapist that enables it to be conveyed and discussed in the language of consciousness and reason. The mutative force arises from the first stage, but if it is not suitably shaped and refined by the second stage, it can lose its beneficial potential or even become damaging to the therapy.

The notion of a relatively dispassionate clinician—however kind and gentle—is, according to this view, a contradiction in terms. The therapeutic encounter simply does not occur without an intense engagement between patient and therapist. Each such impingement is utterly unique. If we take a grand view, then we can say that each such therapeutic event, like all other dyadic experiences, constitutes a micromoment of human history.

The second stage of interpretation shapes and refines the experiences that constitute the first stage. The therapist who is open to the first stage of interpretation carries out the second stage more effectively because much richer psychological data become available.

The concept of countertransference, which assumes that the therapist only reacts to the patient, is too limited for a full understanding of a therapist's idiosyncratic contributions, and it blurs the distinction between the two stages of interpretation. Yet useful interpretations can ensue from the analysis of countertransference, which is usually regarded only as an intermittent interference. Such analysis may incidentally bring new understanding and better interpretation to the therapy. Ultimately, the notion of countertransference derives from the assumption that the origin and cure of the patient's problems are intrapsychic and that any powerful emotional experience on the part of the therapist is reactive and essentially inappropriate. Therefore, the concept of countertransference does connote a problem, which in turn logically suggests that there should be an effort to reduce countertransference. Supposedly, this reduction restores the therapist to a peaceful and undistracted state in which he or she can then attend empathically to the patient. Such assumptions are neither realistic nor desirable. The basic problem inheres in the term countertransference, which is heavily laden with intimations of distortion, blindness, overreaction, and injudicious intervention. Such connotations remain despite the fact that authors such as Little (1951) and Epstein and Feiner (1979) treat countertransference as a normative phenomenon, and therefore an important psychotherapeutic resource.

The term countertransference is still linked to an outdated positivistic view of the analytic process that excludes the subjective world of the analyst. Because, conceptually, countertransference ignores the primary emotional involvement of the analyst, which is a basic element of the therapeutic process, the term is too limiting to represent and convey the fundamental importance and complexity of the analyst's involvement in the process.

Schafer (1983) explicitly accords powerful influence to the analyst's role in the unfolding of treatment. He refers to the "narrative structure" and the "narrative organization" of the analyst without, however, presenting specific examples of how the therapist's "narrative structure" influences therapy. The omission is regrettable. The nondisclosure of such specifics contributes to an unwitting conspiracy of silence among analytic authorities regarding events that are among the most essential elements in the therapeutic process. It also increases the possibility of reification of the expression "narrative structure."

CLINICAL EXAMPLE OF THE TWO STAGES

The following vignette exemplifies the role of the analyst's "narrative structure" in the development of the treatment situation and in the creation of an interpretation.

> L.P. is a professionally successful divorced woman in her middle forties who has two adolescent children, a daughter and a younger son. She entered psychoanalysis with the primary presenting problem of being in love with a homosexual man who had no serious intention of changing his sexual orientation. She also had a chronic weight problem, feelings of inferiority about her intellectual and social abilities, and periodic angry eruptions at her two offspring. Although she had spent many years in analysis and therapy, her ability to free associate was conspicuously limited. During her present analysis, she extricated herself from the hopeless relationship with the homosexual man (they had never been physically intimate). Also, she lost some weight, developed more confidence in her intellectual and social competence, and achieved an improved frustration tolerance with her children.

The following segment of the analysis is offered to demonstrate the intersubjective processes essential to an analysis. First, it illustrates how an ingrained quality of the analyst (my shame over the appearance of my clothing) stimulates analytic behavior in the patient. Second, it elucidates the analyst's subjective response to the patient's analytic actions, and how this response, properly modulated, constitutes a crucial mediatory component in the development of the appropriate interpretations.

> This woman enjoyed an especially fine sense of style. Early in the analysis, she developed a tendency to criticize my way of dressing. Initially, she concentrated on my socks, which she thought were too short, since they exposed some

of my leg to her view as she lay down on or arose from the couch. These were complex communications. She would scold me vigorously, saying that my sloppiness existed in incongruous contrast to my professional skill and efficiency. Since she was very sensitive to her own appearance—particularly her weight—her clothing criticisms often seemed to have the quality of an insecure child defensively devaluing another child. She also enjoyed lecturing me on my lack of tasteful attire. This pleasure was sexualized for her, and she felt it established an erotic bridge between us. Her preoccupation with my clothing engendered a special kind of consciousness in me. As her analytic hours approached, I would become hyperaware of my clothing, and particularly the length of my socks. Her focus on my clothing persisted, spreading to various other aspects of my attire. Her perception that I was combining clashing colors became a frequent source of irritation and amusement for her. Simultaneously, my sartorial confidence dwindled, and in her presence I felt that I had lost my clothing identity. That is, I felt that I was utterly unable to select style or color or fabric with mature taste. Thus I seemed to combine a narcissistic deficit with a continuing sense of professional mastery. It was like an island of self-loss in a sea of adequacy.

Then, a session occurred that brought the matter of my clothing into powerful interpretive focus and ended this pattern of interaction. On the fateful day, I was feeling buoyant, in the belief that I had selected clothes for the day with originality and taste. I was probably exuding a need for recognition and approval. However, when the patient entered my office for her session, she shook her head and smiled wanly in mock despair. She commented, as she reclined on the couch, that this outfit was probably the most poorly selected set of garments she had ever seen on me. She noted that coat, tie, shirt, trousers, socks, and shoes were each of a different color. My sartorial self-esteem evaporated. As usual, however, my overall self-esteem remained intact, even as this isolated area of narcissistic regression occurred. As I recalled my childhood of shoes with rundown heels and worn-out soles, sweaters with missing buttons and holes in the elbows, frayed shirts, worn and baggy trousers, the subjective experience became painful. This island of vulnerability seemed as freshly painful as in childhood, yet I also coolly observed myself during these unpleasant memories. The feelings of shame joined a network of remembered anguish about the ugly house, the ethnic inferiority, the semiliterate and unnaturalized parents, the deviant family radicalism, as well as my unsavory, irrepressible, and largely ungratified sexual desires. Perhaps these specifics sufficiently portray the inner fantasy activity with which I was meeting the patient. I became aware that the development of an important interpretation was underway, although I could not anticipate its precise form.

When the patient completed her slashing critique, her associative attention turned to another man. But this man, like me, older and paternally relevant, had been attacking *her*. She had recently met him at a party and become infatuated. He was worldly, charming, and apparently interested in her. When they were together, however, he severely criticized her behavior and appearance. Although he contended that he was just joking, the patient felt very hurt. After several dates, she confronted him with his lack of sexual assertiveness. He replied that although he could never make love to a fat woman, he would enjoy it if she performed fellatio on him. These remarks devastated her, and she ended the relationship.

I could now adumbrate my interpretation; it was beginning to become a conscious entity, potentially transmissible to the patient. My associations had shifted from my childhood of shame to the patient's early life. I recalled that she believed that her father had always been harshly critical of her appearance and her social behavior. He would frequently erupt with impatient discontent and annoyance. She had longed for his affirmation, but she received only negation. On the other hand, her mother's aggression was more insidious. She did not erupt, nor was she overtly critical of the patient, but the patient felt uneasy with her mother, clung to her, felt unable to have any disagreeable or critical thoughts toward her. Only in young adulthood did she become aware of her mother's submerged hostility and the damage it had done.

Her father was a stylish dresser, who frequented fashionable places such as the Stork Club and Cafe Society Downtown. He was a chic radical, and she recalled with some pride that her father had been denounced as a political subversive to the House Un-American Activities Committee by a celebrated actor, not by some ordinary informer.

In recent weeks she had recalled a family crisis during her puberty when the father decided to leave the mother, which he then did not do. She had felt sexually aroused then, as she imagined him caressing her naked breasts. This arousal recurred in the session as she remembered this fantasy.

The process of interpretation formation was now approaching explication, having moved gradually from the phase of passionate impingement to the stage of conscious formulation. It is this latter stage that is achieved through the professional skill derived from rigorous training and extensive experience. Hence, I could now begin formulating the presumptive psychodynamics.

Various important psychological trends became apparent to me. Primarily, I perceived the crescendo of clothing criticism to be an act of aggression toward me, approximating her father's hostile actions to her. Second, she was repeatedly testing me to confirm and reconfirm that I would not angrily repudiate her as her father so often had. (In this regard, as the patient would snipe at my taste, I would also feel like an ungainly but powerful mastiff being yipped and snapped at by an irritable puppy who counts upon the protective patience of the adult.) Additionally, I was now convinced that the sexual component of the criticisms was linked to father feelings—the clothing being a suitable carrier of the exciting fantasies of nakedness in her father's presence.

I spoke to her in the quiet, professional tones that conformed to the traditional idea of the kind, empathic, calm analyst. My interpretation was that she needed to criticize and ridicule aspects of me just as her father had criticized and ridiculed her in childhood. I specified "identification with the aggressor" as an unconsciously motivated method of attempting to master the old pain. I said further that she attacked me to reconfirm continually my capacity to maintain a caring availability because of a lurking fear that I would lapse into aggression as her father had. And finally, I stated that she teased me in order to re-create the sexual excitement of a fantasied naked encounter with her father.

The patient listened very carefully as I made my comments. She asked some questions to clarify the notion of identifying with the aggressor. She felt that my interpretation helped her understand the importance of her behavior to me in the process of resolving her problems with her parents and the consequent neurotic phenomena. Subsequently, she *never* teased or criticized me for my clothing, although occasionally she would note that I looked nicely attired.

In these interpretations, I provided no verbal indication of the counterpart inner turbulence that I had endured prior to this point. The second, formal stage of the interpretation did not require explicit inclusion of the associative fantasy experience I had undergone, despite the fact that my internal experience constituted the necessary preliminary events from which the final form of the interpretation was derived.

I bring clothing anxiety and shame to my human encounters, and I am particularly aware of these feelings when I am with a person who is stylish and clothes-conscious, as was this patient. When my subjective experience became painful and yet so well delimited, I realized that an intersubjective event of interpretable nature was occurring. My own responses helped me define her own shame over her appearance and her guilt over her sexual feelings, which intensified the shame. This understanding, in turn, easily led me to understand that her teasing and baiting me was derived partly from her identification with the aggressor, her father.

The analysis of my regressive experience (which I carried out silently) enabled me to be undefensive and relatively anxiety free in making my interpretations to her. Without this intervening self-analysis, unconscious defensive motives could easily have colored my remarks and could have stimulated distrust and resistance in the patient.

My personal sensitivity to shame is one of various narrative structures that have influenced my psychological life. I could have selected other examples that would have revealed less profound narcissistic vulnerability, less sexual guilt, less obvious exhibitionistic conflict. My responses, as reported, could readily be assessed as unmistakable countertransference, although to me the term has such parochial connotations that I believe Schafer's (1983) "narrative structure" is more fitting. The latter term indicates characteristics of the therapist that are basic, essential, and powerful, and that may or may not seem "neurotic" according to the values of a particular cultural context. I bring to the treatment the familiar discomfiture of the once depreciated Jewish boy, which to the analytic eye and ear is quite countertransferencelike. Another therapist may experience the treatment with an attitude of unflappable Establishment self-esteem. This subjective state might not be regarded as countertransference, but it will be an equally influential factor in shaping the analysis. In each instance, the therapist is bringing a set of memories, values, and patterns of interpersonal response that can well be called a narrative structure. It is not established that either type of therapist necessarily provides therapeutic work of a superior or inferior quality. In fact, it may simply be that each creates a different set of therapeutic truths. The avid elucidation of these respective truths induces psychological development in both patient and therapist.

4

A NEW DEFINITION OF INTERPRETATION

From the beginning of training, psychotherapists learn that their most powerful tool for change is interpretation. They learn that interpretation provides insight. They learn to gauge patients' responses to interpretation. They learn what, when, and how much to interpret. They are taught to distinguish interpretation from confrontation, advice, clarification, suggestion, manipulation, and reflection. These and many other aspects of interpretation become crucial ingredients of therapists' disciplined activity in the therapeutic encounter.

EXPANDED MEANING

The process of interpretation is a creative one. How is an interpretation constructed? Does it arise primarily from a dispassionate evaluation of the associative data, coolly and skillfully converted into a well-timed and dosed verbalization to the patient? While these constitute the more or less "visible" qualities of interpretation, they are not the elements that provide the truest meaning or the deepest therapeutic power for change in the patient through the act of interpretation.

A broader definition of interpretation in psychotherapy is necessary. The traditional meaning emphasizes the logical, cognitive, dispassionate aspects. But interpretation also includes the emotional, the unconscious, and the sensuous components—as in a musician's interpretation of a piece of music. Sometimes one aspect prevails, and sometimes another. When a therapist talks to the patient, an attempt is being made to effect therapeutic change. A question, a confrontation, or a clarification becomes more than its manifest characteristics; it has occurred only partly because of conscious factors. Its timing, its quality, and its impact also reflect the unconscious experience of the therapist. The importance of the personal, subjective qualities probably exceeds the importance of the formal qualities. One could use the term "interpretation" for all intentional types of therapist interventions. This definitional change would expand analytic attention to include not only the formal characteristics of the therapist's verbalizations, but also the therapist's underlying ideas, which constitute the dynamic subtext.

Ideally, it should be possible to analyze every interpretation into its components: an unconscious event in the therapist that has a conscious surface with a personal meaning, a simultaneous insight in the therapist into the basic meaning of the patient's part in the events that contributed to the therapist's conscious fantasy, a translation of the insight into some intervention by the therapist—the verbal component being the most identifiable and reproducible, but which inevitably includes important nonverbal elements.

For the purpose of this discussion, it is necessary to distinguish between unconscious fantasy and conscious fantasy. Yet this distinction should not be overly sharp and clear.

The unconscious fantasy obviously has to be inferred rather than observed. The usual psychological data, such as one's conscious thoughts and associations, affect, symptoms, and dreams provide the basis for such inference. These inferred unconscious fantasies are the basic dramatic form of the person's passionate motivation. Conscious fantasy, on the other hand, does not require inference. Conscious fantasy exists in consciousness: a person experiences and observes such fantasy; he does not have to infer it. Yet the conscious fantasy does partake of some of the meaning of the unconscious fantasy as an expression of the individual's view of the world. At the same time, conscious fantasy also shares some qualities of an interpretation, inasmuch as it may express ideas about another person. Conscious fantasy, then, exists as a transitional phenomenon of interpretation, mediating the therapist's progression from passionate unconscious fantasy regarding the patient to judiciously formulated interpretation of the patient's therapeutic circumstance.

The patient experiences the interpretation—hears it, sees it (visible but nonverbal ingredients), and feels it (affective component). It is often difficult to know whether the verbal or the nonverbal components have the greater power. Perhaps the impact arises from the very way the verbal and nonverbal elements combine. The interpretation has influence, for good or ill. It, in turn, becomes a tributary that feeds into the patient's current inner experience. A gestalt of psychological events occurs in the patient, some of which become known to the therapist, such as the patient's associations, level of comfort or discomfort, attitude to therapist and therapy, and a host of other nonverbal communications. The patient will also be having a fantasy or memory that may or may not be reported. If it is not directly conveyed, the therapist nevertheless may be able to make an approximate inference as to its nature. This capability of the therapist is enhanced when the therapist realizes that an ongoing joint fantasy links patient and therapist. And the therapist's own fantasy often provides clues about the patient's unreported fantasy. The following vignette illustrates some of these points.

A middle-aged Asian man, a minimalist painter, came for consultation because of an acute eruption of anxiety. He told me that he was the illegitimate son of a politically prominent man in his country of origin and that he had never met his father. As he impassively told me this story I became aware of my own father- and brother-seeking tendencies, and I assumed that unconsciously I was seeking such gratification from the patient. I associated to the fact that on the precise date the patient specified as the time of onset of his anxiety, a man who currently occupied the same public position previously held by the patient's father had committed suicide because of an international scandal. This combination of thoughts suggested to me that the patient was struggling with yearning for his father and that the recent news from his native country had triggered the outbreak of anxiety. I made a tentative interpretation to that effect, but the patient rejected the idea, offering instead the explanation of occupational factors as the cause of his anxiety. The interpretation, which at first glance may seem terribly premature, thereafter evoked a powerful therapeutic process in which the patient dealt with his longings for a father and his resentful feelings to his mother for preventing a relationship between the patient and his natural father.

My intersubjective appraisal is that the patient and I approached one another with related underlying fantasy expectations: finding a father. These fantasies interacted powerfully; I became aware of father-seeking feelings and had the association to the relevant political event mentioned above. I was able to infer a psychological meaning for the patient's symptom, and I then constructed the interpretation.

Although the patient is usually the more active overt communicator, the informed therapist will not dismiss his or her own ongoing fantasies as neurotic countertransference. The therapist will understand his or her shift of feelings, the accompanying fantasy, and the change of attitude toward the patient as, of course, reflecting the therapist's idiosyncratic needs. But they are also a reflection—and perhaps the best available one—of the patient's most immediate and acute picture of himself. They are an expression of the joint fantasy being created continuously by patient and therapist. These three entities are, in the heat of immediate experience, not readily distinguishable or divisible. Valid analytical separation can occur at later, more reflective moments. During the therapeutic transaction, authentic participation precludes ongoing sorting and classifying, which would vitiate the intimate quality and cause the loss of the heuristic and creative opportunity.

Optimal involvement with the patient requires that the therapist maintain an overarching, ambiguous stance. In this way the therapist can readily cope with, and even welcome, the occurrence of contradictions and inconsistencies in the patient and in himself. Out of this capacity arises the ability to achieve unexpected insights and to generate novel interpretations. Thus the zest for ambiguity (or at least a tolerance of it) becomes an indispensable trait of a sophisticated therapist.

Regardless of theoretical orientation, the therapist must maintain maximal openness to self and other during the therapeutic encounter. The achievement of a simultaneous appreciation of one's own immediate needs, the patient's self-portrait, and the new jointly created psychological meaning requires that the therapist relinquish a sense of separateness and release himself to the swirling currents of interaction and meaning. In this state, the therapist lives through profound emotional events, including intense fear, as well as resentment, despair, and excitement. An overarching confidence in a creative outcome sustains the therapist—and the therapy—during this turbulent sequence of events.

This vivid picture of creative chaos does not invalidate the traditional understanding of the construction, conveyance, and consequence of interpretation. It does indicate, however, that an exclusive focus upon the formal, verbal aspect of interpretation is too narrow. In many instances, this narrowness may coexist with a favorable result, although the basic mutative factors may be misconstrued or overlooked. Alternatively, the therapist utters the "correct" ideas but conveys inappropriate and negating nonverbal messages by tone of voice, choice of words, facial expression, posture, gestures, and related signals. The patient's reactions are to the latter communications (the subtext), but the therapist may defensively continue to attend only to the verbal "correctness" of the interpretation. Circumstances like these indicate why interpretation should be defined as the total communication and why the nonexplicit components of interpretation should be known to the interpreter.

The expansion of the scope of interpretation clashes with an excessive physical science orientation to psychoanalytic therapy, which leads to pseudoscientific confusion and disorder. Leites (1971) has shown how the muddy meanings of so many of our terms render fact and conjecture indistinguishable. For example, consider the notion of a basic model technique. Ostensibly, this technique strives for and achieves a purity akin to the aseptic technique of surgery or the experimental method of basic research, in which all the possibly interfering variables are controlled. Actually, adherence to this basic model technique would exclude the very elements of intervention that are basic to effective therapy. With this technique, an interpretation would be utterly dispassionate (rather than passionate), would be stripped of idiosyncratic emphasis or quality of any kind, and would rely solely on its cognitive power. A therapist who adheres to a physical science model of therapy would not find a broadened view of interpretation at all congenial.

I am not necessarily arguing against the notion of psychoanalysis and psychotherapy as science, since one might argue for the scientific purpose of my recommendations. They are, after all, intended to expose and define hitherto unacknowledged variables of great influence upon the therapeutic process in order to increase awareness of the richness of therapeutic events.

The unutterably complex nature of the human encounter precludes any possible approximation of an ideal technique. A therapist who strives for it, and fails, will suffer continually from a professional guilt that will impair his or her therapeutic availability. On the other hand, if a therapist believes that he or she has in fact achieved this scientific ideal, that belief can be maintained only through continuous denial of the inconvenient but indispensable complexities. Denial will also impoverish therapeutic responsiveness. Striving for a coherent, consistent theory upon which technique can be confidently based does not facilitate analytic work, and in fact recent developments in psychoanalytic theory have fortunately contained and tempered these tendencies.

Freud was strikingly vague in spelling out the details of psychoanalytic technique. He knew that analysis of the analyst did more than simply eliminate quirks that would interfere with the analyst's detached pursuit of the patient's unconscious conflicts. More important, it enables the analyst's subjective life to have an enlarged constructive influence in the shaping of the analyst's work with patients. Otherwise, this influence may remain dissociated and may even become damaging. A broader intersubjective view of the psychoanalytic process that includes a consistent appreciation of the analyst's or therapist's continuous subjective contribution does not permit retention of the sharply delineated, traditional definition of interpretation.

How does the expansion of the definition of interpretation correlate with the primacy of verbal formulation in psychotherapy and its conveyance via the spoken word? The pressure in psychodynamic therapy has always been toward increased consciousness of one's own psychological experience. And this consciousness exists in close, although not entirely consistent, relation to the ability to formulate one's self in verbal terms. Therefore, it is logical to expect the effective therapist to be a master of verbal communication and to have a correspondingly rich appreciation of the subtle powers of such discourse. Furthermore, one might reasonably expect the therapist to rely primarily upon verbal interventions that attempt to illuminate psychological meaning through logic and reason, that is, through interpretation as traditionally defined in psychotherapy.

Reasoned thoughts have a very important role in psychotherapy and psychotherapeutic interpretations. However, optimal self-definition and self-actualization cannot be achieved solely through a series of preliminary verbal insights derived from the explicit ideas contained in the interpretations offered by the therapist. This is only one part of the pattern of growth.

In actuality, insight often occurs in a flash, as a surprise (Reik 1948). Life events that lead to verbal and nonverbal insight are often realistically or symbolically powerful experiences, without a significant accompanying verbal commentary. The learning and discovery value inhere in the very experience itself. Verbal explication in the course of the experience may sometimes disrupt and thus attenuate the mutative power of the experience. The generally accepted approach to the timing of interpretations supports these assertions. Therapists often defer interpretations because they judge the moment not to be propitious.

Several years ago, one of those uniquely psychotherapeutic dramas occurred in my practice. Among its other instructive qualities, the experience provides a vivid illustration of the relevance of timing in psychotherapic interventions.

A single man in his early forties had been in psychotherapy for over a year. At the outset of treatment he was anxious, depressed, and excessively inhibited. He also was unhappy in his career as an investment banker.

We began treatment with much talk of his frustrating present and its apparent relation to his very unhappy past. He was one of three children of an impoverished Irish–American family. His mother died in his infancy and his father had been unable to provide sufficient parenting at any time in the patient's development.

After the first month of therapy, the patient felt that my commitment to him was firm. At that point he was able to reveal that he felt compelled to cruise the streets of Hollywood, picking up young male hustlers, taking them to a motel or other secluded spot, and having manual, oral, or anal sex with them. This revelation, although surprising, did not seem incongruous with his total personality and symptomatic picture or with his developmental traumas. His conscious perception of his sexual identity remained heterosexual, and I, too, continued to regard him as fundamentally heterosexual.

I was able to integrate his disclosures into my interpretive themes, which dealt largely with the vicissitudes of his present life as partial manifestation of the disorganizing effects of childhood experiences. His sexual practice was addressed as an erotized organizing function, helping him maintain a semblance of intactness of his self. The varied transference manifestations were considered within the same conceptual framework. He and I shared the impression that a slow but steady therapeutic process was evolving.

Then the news of AIDS came upon us, shattering the therapeutic tranquility. I realized the terrible risks he assumed when he went cruising, while he seemed relatively unconcerned about the dangers of infection. My attitude toward his sexual behavior changed drastically, and I could no longer maintain my previous nondirective interest. Instead, when he reported that he had gone cruising, I would interrupt my listening and associating. I would become worried and express my concern to him. He would demand that I resume my previous analytic, accepting stance. I would refuse, telling him that I would not do so until he stopped cruising. He would accuse me of not being a real analyst, and I would rejoin that he was expecting me to behave like Nero during the great conflagration. This became an impasse for a period of one or two months. I sought consultation and received encouragement to maintain the focus on the extremely dangerous path he was following. His opposition subsided, and he grudgingly promised to restrict his adventures to looking and being looked at, with no touching, and above all with no exposure to the other person's body fluids.

Much time has elapsed, many changes have occurred. He no longer seeks promiscuous homosexual gratification, although some desire persists. I no longer assume an alter ego function. His clinical health is good and he is HIV negative. We have resumed more typical therapeutic transactions because it is now timely to do so.

What an ironic situation! A patient who ostensibly is highly motivated wants his therapist to make profound, subtle interpretations of his acting out in relation to his fantasies about the therapist and their relation to the past, without any negative intimations. The therapist insists that the timing is dangerously wrong for such an approach, which can only be undertaken when there is some reliable evidence that the grave risks are being avoided. Instead, the therapist avers, only interpretations carrying an urgent warning of self-destructive meanings are possible at this time.

Let me offer a list of hypothetical interventions by a therapist, progressing from less to greater verbal explication of the presumed problem. Each in its own way is an interpretive comment, reflecting the appropriate level of verbalization at the particular time. As the preliminary work progresses, it becomes more timely to make increasingly explicit remarks, such as these:

1. The therapist shakes his or her head in silent expression of how difficult this situation must be for the patient.

2. The therapist verbally acknowledges the patient's painful experience and may encourage the patient to say more about it.

3. The therapist comments that the patient now seems more able to express more of the total inner feeling about this very difficult problem.

4. The therapist indicates that there are probably more fundamental conflicted matters attached to the immediate preoccupations, but they are not yet crystallized enough for specific address.

These responses, each verbally more complex than the preceding one, share a concern about time and timing. And their common latent premise is that it is not yet timely to discuss the basic psychological meaning of the presenting problem. In this sense, even the relatively simple silent shaking of the head, which the therapist intuitively *and* consciously substitutes for a verbal response, is a silent communication of an idea and an attitude from therapist to patient. In the subtext, the therapist is saying, "I am convinced that other matters which are not yet part of our dialogue are highly influential in this present problem, yet I believe that you are still too vulnerable for frank discussion; hence I do not feel optimal comfort in mentioning them to you. We can wait for a more propitious moment, and in the meantime, my empathic head movements and facial expression demonstrate my confidence that you will comprehend and master the problem in due time." This essential message of responsive delay and simultaneous basic confidence informs each of the variations mentioned. The fourth variation obviously is a more overt expression of these ideas. The seeming paradox is that while verbal consciousness represents the most complete achievement of psychological understanding, the timely steps taken on the path to this result may sometimes require either nonverbal means or verbal behavior that temporarily excludes explication of the presumed fundamental problem. Yet these indirect, implicit, or nonverbal interventions may constitute essential preliminary ingredients that ultimately result in the full verbal elucidation of the basic truths. Premature verbal presentation may well diminish the possibility of the most complete and desirable consciousness.

Psychotherapy may in one sense be regarded as a continuous dialectical interplay of the implicit and the explicit. In part, this is the same as the relationship between the unconscious and the conscious. The difference in these polarities is primarily that one, the implicit–explicit, is interpersonal, and the other, the unconscious–conscious, is intrapsychic. They are different dimensions of experience. Neither is subordinate or superordinate to the other, although implication–explication is the broader of the two, and it subsumes the other within it. An implication may exist within an interpretation and be unconscious to the interpreter. Here repression may be operating. However, the implicit may also be a matter of choice. In the hypothetical example cited above, the therapist was *choosing* to express the preliminary interpretive messages through implication. The choice itself, while obviously not entirely based upon conscious considerations, did nevertheless include an awareness of the basic formulation and a judgment (right or wrong) that full explication was inappropriate. The interpenetrating influence of implicit–explicit and unconscious–conscious activity continuously codetermine the relative proportions of verbal and nonverbal components in the interpretive interventions of the therapist. It is very unlikely that purely verbally explicit interpretations are ever possible, let alone useful, in psychotherapy.

INTERPRETATION IN THE THERAPEUTIC PROCESS

Kohut, Lacan, and numerous other constructive critics of psychoanalysis have helped prepare us for radical reexamination of interpretation. Such a reappraisal should lead to an enriched appreciation of the originating elements and processes that produce an interpretation, and result in a corresponding enhancement of an interpretation's full influence upon the person to whom it is addressed and delivered. While an interpretation may be, to a limited degree, perceived and explored as though it were a discrete and autonomous entity, it must also be regarded as a nodal moment in an ongoing interpersonal process. An interpretation's basic meaning may change as the psychotherapeutic process unfolds. And many of its characteristics, such as form, intensity, emphatic quality, mutative power, emotional coloration, blatancy or subtlety, may undergo continuous transformation as the psychological field changes with time. This process will reflect ongoing changes in the inner world of both therapist and patient.

These complexities may help us understand why therapist and patient often experience interpretations quite differently. For example, a therapist may offer an interpretation with a strong belief that the crucial insight therein will liberate the patient from some chronic debilitating anxiety, only to discover with chagrin that the patient's primary appraisal was that the interpretation was a self-serving act by the therapist, serving a defensive purpose. Here is an example. A rigid male therapist was working with a woman who developed strong sexual feelings toward him. She began to blandish him in a blatantly erotic way. The therapist construed these communications as acting out and told the patient so. The patient was deeply hurt and bewildered by this tactless comment. The therapist, of course, was oblivious to the fact that he had acted out to ward off his own anxiety. Similarly, haven't therapists often made an interpretation with enthusiasm and at a later time reflected on the event with embarrassed appreciation of its narcissistic motivation?

A liberal but still conventional definition is that "an interpretation is a statement that conveys the latent meaning of the patient's thoughts, feelings, actions. This communication of knowledge from therapist to patient is more than a cognitive event; it is inseparable from the total therapeutic relationship. The purpose of an interpretation is to enhance the self understanding and self awareness of the patient, which then leads to conflict resolution. Interpretation is offered when the patient is ready and receptive—although this may not always be obvious" (Natterson 1986, p. 309). But although I think this definition is useful and valid, it has deficiencies requiring discussion.

This simple definition becomes clearer and more complete if one elucidates the large areas of ambiguity it contains. For instance, the ambiguous reference to the "total therapeutic relationship" indicates that imbedded in the subtext of an interpretation are the significant psychological events occurring in the therapist that contribute to or result from the activities which create the interpretation. Also, reference to "when the patient is ready and receptive . . ." is vague, but points to the question of timing, the current quality of relatedness of the two parties, and the level of resistance in each person. These are important areas of meaning in interpretation that are often not attended to.

Interpretations should be framed as working hypotheses by a friendly, nonauthoritarian therapist. Within this framework, much stylistic variation exists from therapist to therapist, and from patient to patient with the same therapist. Style is an important matter in interpretation. It may, of course, validly reflect the inner state of the therapist and the quality of the therapeutic relationship, but this is not always the case. A therapist who is parsimonious with words may be quite generous with emotion and allusion. A therapist with an ingratiating style suggesting a democratic attitude may in fact be concealing an authoritarian orientation. Stylistic qualities that conceal antihumanistic tendencies can induce a disruptive and damaging dissonance in the patient. The capacity for a searching, creative openness versus the tendency to defensive closure varies from moment to moment in each party in therapy, and this continuous variation is partly dependent upon the influence of each on the other.

The stylistic variations are complex phenomena derived from the totality of life experience of the therapist. As the therapist becomes deeply involved in the therapeutic process, he or she cannot remain detached. The therapist's stylistic variations will reflect shifts in subjective experience of the patient. Specific memories, yearnings, expectations, discomforts, and defenses characterize the therapist's subjective involvement at each moment. Optimally, the therapist will be continuously "open" to these inner experiences, but his or her attention to them will fluctuate. This fluctuating attention is neither random nor inaccessible to reflection. Sustained sensitive scrutiny enables therapists to understand when and why their attention turns toward or away from their subjective experience. The various meanings of such attentional shifts are discussed in the chapter on therapist self-scrutiny.

Decisions by the therapist to be tentative or definite, terse or lengthy, crisp or rambling, clear or vague, cool or tender, loud or faint, are all derived from complex psychological events, only partly conscious, that are part of the therapeutic process as mediated by the therapist's subjective experience. To lump such modal choices under the heading of "the art of therapy" would be a reification and would stifle more complete discovery of meaning. Instead, each such choice deserves detailed examination.

Therapists' styles are probably endlessly varied, except for those therapists whose unconscious conflicts are so untouched that they develop a defensive rigidity that becomes their trademark. More usual is a suppleness that permits appropriate changes from patient to patient but that still derives in part from the therapist's own history and subjectivity. For example, a depressed middle-aged "mogul" tells me that my approach to him is like that of a prizefighter. I await my opportunity, then I move in, pounding at him relentlessly. On the other hand, a 38-year-old female Ph.D. candidate in psychology assures me that I am gently attuned to her needs. She says that she feels completely safe with me, and never experiences any jarring impact from me. Each of these patients doubtless perceives me in a way that is congruent with his or her subjective need, yet I am equally certain that my style differs in these two cases. The man, as a child, was seriously neglected by his mother, and my punching stance with him involves both our experiences of neglect. The woman suffered sexual molestation by her father when she was 3 years old. My finely tuned approach to her meets her specific needs for a loving respect, but my similar needs are thus also conveyed to her. I believe that my desire for intimacy drives me in both these clinical situations, but my differing style in each case is created by the specific interaction of the patient's deep unconscious need with my own.

Interpretations involve the patient's passionate existence, both interior and interpersonal. The interpretation is addressed to the life issues of the patient, such as fantasy life, self-concept, significant ongoing relationships (especially the patient–therapist relationship), or connections between present and past life experiences. The effective therapist will continuously accord full importance to these aspects of interpretive intervention. In addition, the therapist must uninterruptedly deal with another agenda of like nature that in the psychotherapeutic dialogue is silent, but that occurs intensely within the therapist. This experience, a kind of subordinated self-analysis, is a crucial component of the therapeutic process. The therapist's fantasies, memories, self preoccupations, and concerns about other people—including other patients—that overlap the therapeutic encounter derive from two separate but convergent sources. One is the overall psychological condition of the therapist, that is, the major conflictual, adaptive, and developmental foci of the therapist's current life. The other source is more specifically stimulated by the patient's life problems that are actively influencing the therapy. The effective therapist treats this usually interpersonally silent agenda (which sometimes can and should be an open component of the dialogue) as an indispensable ingredient in the therapist's appropriate understanding, empathy, and intervention.

An optimal psychotherapeutic process consists of an endless sequence of patient–therapist transactions, each unique and largely subtextual. These important ingredients cannot be adequately subsumed to the assumptions and language we usually employ in a discussion of interpretation. Despite the difficulties presented by the uniqueness and complexity of each psychotherapeutic moment, a comprehensive discussion of interpretation is possible. This approach acknowledges the impossibility of a completely systematized method of construction and delivering interpretations. It maintains that an open, ambiguous stance toward interpretation is the most effective. Each interpretation is unique—yet there are similarities enough to permit us to categorize or classify interpretations.

5

FROM COUNTERTRANSFERENCE TO INTERSUBJECTIVITY

Countertransference, while never a warmly received member of the family of psychodynamic concepts, has always been exceedingly useful. During the first half of this century, countertransference was officially treated as an undesirable albeit frequent therapeutic contaminant, and yet ironically it became a widely used resource for therapeutic understanding. This attitude has evolved into a general acceptance of countertransference as a normative phenomenon, but it also retains its pathological implications. Such an admixture of conflicting meanings is not helpful to therapists. New ways of looking at the analyst's subjectivity now seem timely. The following review of important ideas about countertransference may illustrate both the problems and the possibilities.

Countertransference has never been a clearly definable phenomenon. Freud (1910a) originally offered the term to account for the analyst's transference reactions that were engendered by the particular analytic situation.

We have become aware of the "counter-transference" which arises in him [the psychoanalyst] as a result of the patient's influence on his unconscious feelings, and we are almost inclined to insist that he recognize this counter-transference in himself and overcome it. Now that a considerable number of people are practising psychoanalysis and exchanging their observations with one another, we have noticed that no psychoanalyst goes further than his own complexes and internal resistances permit; and we consequently require that he shall begin his activity with a self-analysis and continually carry it deeper while he is making his observations on his patients. [pp. 144–145]

At best, these reactions would be intermittent, and they would be quantitatively manageable and qualitatively benign. The analyst's significant, powerful human reactions had to be treated as at least a potential detriment in order for a theory focused on the intrapsychic world of the analysand to remain tenable. While effective psychoanalysts have always used their inner experience as a vital ingredient in the analytic process, they have been somewhat reluctant to acknowledge this. When they have discussed such phenomena, they have done so in terms of countertransference. This reticence has arisen from guilt over deviation from the state of neutrality and detachment prescribed by the classical theory of technique.

The evolution of countertransference has occurred in three important steps: countertransference as

1. disruptive, destructive, with its detection and elimination being necessary to relieve blockage of the therapy,

2. neurotic and potentially damaging if not analyzed and eliminated (or reduced); but often providing therapeutic understanding of basic importance, thereby adding greatly to the progress of the therapy,

3. a normative phenomenon; every therapist has abundant idiosyncratic responses to every patient, which play a fundamental part in the shape and course of the therapeutic events.

Although even today not all therapists would accept this third stage as valid, long experience of many therapists with treatment, supervision, and clinical case instruction have made the third stage increasingly popular. Some call this the *totalist* position.

Can the therapist's intense, influential, insight-providing, personal experiences still be adequately defined by the term "countertransference"? The study of this question indicates the necessity for an alternative concept.

The basic issue is whether the therapist's psychological involvement in therapy is spontaneous and initiating or reactive and secondary. The way in which it is defined, named, valued, and approached will flow from how it is perceived. The purely intrapsychic theory of psychoanalysis deliberately excludes the human transactional component, insists that the optimal analyst only reacts to the analysand, and maintains that idiosyncratic phenomena in the analyst are essentially reactive to the analysis and need to be kept to a minimum. This point of view justifies the term countertransference, and it preserves the intrapsychic theory of cause and cure.

Classical psychoanalytic writers have not consistently adhered to this negative approach to countertransference, however. The stages of countertransference development represent an important, but not exclusive, trend in the approach to the analyst's psychological role. Freud (1912) stated that the analyst ". . . must turn his own unconscious like a receptive organ to the transmitting unconscious of the patient. He must adjust himself to the patient as a telephone receiver is adjusted to the transmitting microphone" (p. 115). And in the same paper, he also wrote, ". . . if the doctor is to be in a position to use his unconscious in this way as an *instrument, . . .* He may not tolerate any resistances in himself which hold back from his consciousness what has been perceived by his unconscious . . ." (p. 116).

Here Freud is requiring the active involvement of the analyst's unconscious as a continuous and crucial component of the analytic process. While the analogy is to an impersonal and noninitiating "organ" or "receiver," the unconscious life of the analyst is neither an organ nor a receiver, and Freud of course knew this. But in this same article, he stated: "The doctor should be opaque to his patients and, like a mirror, should show them nothing but what is shown to him" (p. 118). And he concluded: "I cannot advise my colleagues too urgently to model themselves during psychoanalytic treatment on the surgeon, who puts aside all his feelings, even his human sympathy, and concentrates his mental forces on the single aim of performing the operation as skillfully as possible" (p. 118).

These quotations demonstrate a fundamental contradiction. Clearly Freud is suggesting that the analyst be like a surgeon, a mirror, an instrument; yet at the same time the analyst should react with his own unconscious to the patient. Freud thus seems to suggest a simultaneous exclusion and inclusion of the analyst's subjective, emotional, and psychological life.

With the introduction of the analyst's psychological life—that is, his or her unconscious—into the analytic process, Freud confuses the issue, because he has now postulated two kinds of unconscious contributions by the analyst: one from the drive-motivated and conflict-shaped countertransference, the other from the nondriven, therapeutic organ–receiver. Perhaps a case could be made for such a dichotomy, but I believe it impairs the development of a unified theory of the analyst's relevant subjectivity. Freud realized intuitively the importance of the analyst's idiosyncratic contribution to the analytic process, but he could not simply acknowledge this without turning to an "interpersonal" theory. Freud was quite rigid in his insistence upon the intrapsychic origins of neurosis and the recapitulation of this intrapsychic process during psychoanalytic treatment. Hence, according to his theory, no fundamental causal role could be played by significant others.

Isakower (1957–1963), in an unpublished work, is reported by others to have carried Freud's idea of a telephone receiver much further. According to Jacobs (1985), it is clear that for Isakower the essence of the analyzing instrument is a particular state of mind experienced by both analyst and analysand. Central to this mental set is a variable degree of regression in both participants. This state of regression, which is a necessary condition in patient and analyst alike for understanding the unconscious communication of the other, is closely allied to the kind of ego regression that occurs in the artist during moments of creative activity. For Isakower, analysis was an art, and his mode of perception in the analytic hours was that of an artist.

Malcove (1975) states that Isakower, following Freud's metaphor of the receiver, introduced the concept of the analyzing instrument. She reports: "Dr. Isakower was asked if he really thought of the analyzing instrument as an entity or did he not consider it to be a metaphor. Dr. Isakower conceded that it could be between an entity and a metaphor. Further study would be needed for the answer, he concluded" (p. 7). Malcove proceeds with her report of Isakower's views:

The analyzing instrument was defined as a teamstructure characterized by its being:

(1) A unique setting in relation to an analogous constellation in a second person.

(2) A protem activated state in rapport with its counterpart in the analysand.

(3) An ad hoc assembly, of a transitory nature, for a special task.

(4) A composite consisting of two complementary halves; both halves functioning together as one in continuous communication.

(5) A relationship of two people in an analogous or nearidentity quality of wakefulness; *not* an identification. [p. 7]

Further, Malcove writes: "Dr. Isakower stresses the importance for the analyst of increasing his *capacity* for *selfobservation* even as the analysand is encouraged to do so. He urges the analyst to heed all of his inner perceptions as valuable percepts and encourages him to use them, be they phrases, images, fantasies or words; to use them in whatever way he considers appropriate in the analytic situation" (p. 8).

Two features of Malcove's paper are additionally noteworthy. First, she makes no reference to countertransference in her discussion of the analyzing instrument. This omission was necessary; otherwise, the traditional pathological connotation of countertransference would have required that the free use of the analyst's unconscious in the analysis be questioned. How would one determine whether these inner perceptions are creative responses or damaging neurotic imposition? She avoids the problem by not mentioning countertransference. Second, the precursors of intersubjectivity are contained in Isakower's notion of the analyzing instrument. Obviously, a "teamstructure" must suggest what is currently called "experience nearness," and it specifically calls for an ongoing, continuous, powerful attunement of the unconscious, emotional experience of both parties.

Later, Stone (1961), Zetzel (1956), and Greenson (1965) dealt with the necessary employment of the personal qualities of the analyst to create a human, rather than a machinelike, climate in the analysis. They shared a recognition that the analyst was not a tabula rasa, and they warned against the damaging effects of efforts to be one. Stone recommended a reduction in the austerity of technique. Zetzel and Greenson proposed the concepts of "therapeutic alliance" and "working relationship," which they attempted, without complete success, to distinguish from transference–countertransference processes.

It would appear that analysts were obliged to find an increasing number of terms to describe and explain a growing awareness of subtle but powerful personal elements contributed by the analyst to the analytic encounter. The phenomenon of countertransference, however, always constituted a threat to these new concepts, which rested on a base of presumed benign, nonidiosyncratic subjectivity. Otherwise, by traditional consensus, they partake of a *neurotic* subjectivity, are *countertransferential,* and damage the analysis. When Loewald (1960) described the necessity of the analyst's regressing with the analysand in the analytic process, he did not confront the problem of the analyst's neurotic elements being thereby activated. Does he mean that analysis must involve the countertransference to be effective? If so, does Loewald really mean countertransference, or is he really referring to the singular subjective component that is spontaneously contributed by the analyst?

In the 1970s, the third, and possibly final, stage of countertransference culminated with the publication of the collection called *Countertransference,* edited by Epstein and Feiner (1979). Countertransference now became healthy, desirable, normal. Countertransference is ever-present and always relevant to and influential in the therapeutic process. It is a valuable resource for therapeutic understanding, but the therapist must look for and understand it. Otherwise, the results of countertransference may become deleterious, because important subjective aspects of the therapist's experience, if repressed, may generate resistance from the therapist's side.

Just as the term *transference* outgrew its original meaning and now possesses more and different meanings, the concept of countertransference has also achieved multiple new meanings. It no longer simply designates a specific transference in the therapist to the patient deriving from past unresolved, unconscious neurotic conflicts of the analyst. It has become more complex and subtle, inseparable from the character, values, attitudes, and interactional style of the therapist. Some aspects are specifically reactive to the patient, but other aspects are independent of the particular patient. Although it has lost much of its original meaning, the term continues to be used from tradition and from habit. The problem is that its continued use prevents questioning of the theoretical assumptions upon which it is based.

Many writers have advocated a more liberal definition and utilization of countertransference. Epstein and Feiner (1979) note: "These two thematic strands—countertransference as a hindrance, and the doctor's use of his own unconscious to understand the patient—have intertwined, like a double helix, throughout the historical development of psychoanalytic conceptions of the countertransference. And, we might add, of its theory of treatment itself" (p. 1). According to the authors, "it was Heimann, Little, Winnicott, and Racker who actually broke through the prevailing classical view that countertransference was simply a hindrance to effective psychoanalytic work" (p. 1).

Paula Heimann (1950) wrote: "The aim of the analyst's own analysis . . . is not to turn him into a mechanical brain which can produce interpretations on the basis of a purely intellectual procedure, but to enable him to sustain the feelings which are stirred in him, as opposed to discharging them (as does the patient), in order to subordinate them to the analytic task in which he functions as the patient's mirror reflection" (p. 82). Heimann in the same paper broadened the definition of countertransference to include all the analyst's emotional reactions to the patient, not only the pathological components.

Margaret Little (1951) noted: "What comes (from the patient) may on occasion be a piece of real countertransference interpretation for the analyst" (p. 39). She also regarded the analyst's unconscious countertransference as a significant influence on the patient's transference as well as the conscious, intentional actions of the analyst.

Winnicott (1958) differentiates three aspects of countertransference:

1. Abnormality in countertransference, and set relationships and identifications that are under repression in the analyst . . . it is evident here, that the analyst needs more analysis.

2. The identifications and tendencies belonging to an analyst's personal experiences and personal development which provide the positive setting for his analytic work and make his work different in quality from that of any other analyst.

3. The truly objective, or the analyst's love and hate in reaction to the actual personality and behavior of the patient based on objective observation.

While Winnicott does not convincingly distinguish each of the types from the other two, there is a distinct difference of emphasis in each, and he certainly indicates that the emotional life of the analyst invariably contributes to the shape and course of the analysis.

Winnicott's work advances our understanding of the therapist's subjectivity by emphasizing that countertransference informs us of the therapist's ongoing psychological processes, and thus becomes a valuable source of information rather than a hindrance. Ironically, work such as Winnicott's, which broadens the concept of countertransference, also undermines it by blurring the strict categorical lines. The idea becomes looser and spongier, ultimately requiring a return to a strict and limiting definition, or possible replacement by some new concept(s). At present, the term countertransference is loaded with new meanings, some of which have very little relation to its original meaning. As the term is employed today, it refers increasingly to all of the analyst's emotional reactions and contributions to the analytic situation.

Racker (1968) contributed the concept of direct and indirect countertransference. *Direct countertransference* is the response of the therapist to the patient, whereas *indirect countertransference* is the therapist's response to some individual outside the analytic situation. Further, Racker subdivides the direct type into (1) *concordant identification,* which occurs when the analyst responds empathically to the patient, and (2) *complementary identification,* wherein the analyst experiences, usually painfully, the patient's projection of unacceptable aspects of himself or herself onto (or into) the therapist. The analyst manages to contain these projections, instead of retaliating in kind. This enables the analyst to achieve a more comprehensive and profound awareness of the therapeutic events, and then to produce more effective interpretation.

In contrast to these advocates of a more liberal definition and utilization of countertransference, others, such as Annie Reich (1973), have held fast to a traditional approach to the definition and employment of countertransference. Such views, while no longer dominant, remain a significant influence on psychoanalytic practice and education. Countertransference was originally postulated to account for the inconvenient presence in the analytic field of personal thoughts and feelings of the analyst that were too powerful and blatant to be disregarded or dismissed.

Tansey and Burke (1989) offer a new, sophisticated exploration of the patterns of subjective interplay of therapist and patient. Relying heavily on a modern, transformed concept of projective identification, they venture a systematic account of the events that establish a link among counter-transference, projective identification, and empathy through the activation of an identificatory experience in the therapist. They state: "Psychoanalytic psychotherapy is a process in which the therapist is susceptible to the full range of human emotions" (p. 203). Although this is a cautious summary statement, the authors show throughout their book that the therapist's subjective involvement is indispensable and in-evitable.

Clearly, the trend has been to regard these subjective reactions increasingly as inescapable, natural, and helpful. The achievement of this view of countertransference neces-sitates revision of the classical Freudian concept of therapeutic action, in which the analyst involves himself in a kind but detached way.

Countertransference as a concept is still too tightly linked to its original meaning of an unconscious pathological response of the analyst to the analysand. Therefore, new terms which acknowledge that the analyst initiates as well as reacts are now required. The language of *intersubjectivity* seems best suited to meet this current need. In this way, countertransference will continue to be a useful term, but within the limits of its original meaning.

6

INTERSUBJECTIVITY VERSUS SELF PSYCHOLOGY

The intersubjective and the implicit are related qualities of exceptional interest in the reappraisal of interpretation. The implicit in psychoanalysis and psychotherapy includes the subtextual, the unexpressed, the alluded to, the indirectly referred to, the consciously suppressed, and the repressed. Implicitness partakes of the same open, fluid theoretical possibilities that also inhere in the concepts of ambiguity and intersubjectivity. Implicitness is crucial to a reconsideration of interpretation because it provides part of an overarching frame of reference to replace the limiting structure provided by the instinct theory and countertransference theory.

Emotionally and psychologically, that which is implicit can be quite precise, but the precision does not become rigid since it is free of a tight linkage to verbal expression. An attitude can be very clear and precise but not accessible to verbal representation; it may be conveyed only implicitly, and yet its exact meaning is unmistakable to both the sender and the receiver.

Because the theoretical basis for psychodynamics has not yet provided another concept, countertransference has come to include all the analyst's subjective involvement in the analysis, with all its qualities of implicitness. But the concept of countertransference also refers to an inappropriate reaction by the analyst, therefore requiring the vitiating notion of the split analyst, who, on the one hand, is objective and dispassionate, but who, on the other hand, is neurotically vulnerable. This analyst's unpredictable unconscious is thus an ever-present source of danger to the treatment of the patient, but it is also capable of yielding valuable analytic understanding. There is a need, in my view, for a better theory that accords major importance to the analyst's subjectivity from the outset of the analysis. Such a theory would necessarily entail abandonment of the instinct drive theory that focuses exclusively on the intrapsychic process. Freud adhered to this instinct theory, and so did his followers. However, during subsequent decades, important contributions to the theory and practice of interpretation have been developed within the framework of classical thinking and have provided some acceptance of the analyst's subjectivity. Cumbersome and unconvincing explanations have attempted to contain such changes within classical theory.

The important papers after Freud by Glover, Strachey, and Loewenstein were each in their own way instructive milestones. These authors recognized that existing theory did not adequately explain how interpretation works, and helped to pave the way for the construction of a theory that would ultimately include the real relationship of the analyst and the analysand, the ongoing unconscious life of the analyst, and the understanding of interpretation as occurring in an intersubjective field.

Glover (1931) attempted to contain the complexities and ambiguities of interpretation within the instinct–drive theory of neurosis. He asked how or whether interpretations were

effective in the earlier periods of analysis prior to discovery
of new phantasy systems that enlarged understanding of unconscious processes. What really happened, he asked, in those
analyses conducted prior to newer knowledge? They were
regarded as successful analyses, but the success was achieved
without the benefit of later advances in psychoanalytic understanding and techniques. To Glover, the interpretations
of the earlier period were perforce inexact and incomplete.
His explanation of how such inexact interpretations work
was as follows: although they do not address the aim or
affect of specific drive-motivated fantasies, or do not refer
even to deeper fantasies, which are central to the patient's
neurosis, these inexact interpretations nevertheless address
some related fantasies and, by contiguity, give some relief
to the patient:

> . . . if we remember that neuroses are spontaneous attempts
> at self-healing, it seems probable that the mental apparatus
> turns at any rate some inexact interpretations to advantage,
> in the sense of substitution products. If we study the element
> of displacement in phobias and obsessions, we are justified
> in describing the state of affairs by saying that the patient
> unconsciously and consciously lives up to an inexact inter-
> pretation of the source of anxiety. It seems plausible, there-
> fore, that another factor is operative in the cure of cases where
> specific phantasy systems are unknown: *viz.* that the patient
> seizes upon the inexact interpretation and converts it into a
> displacement-substitute. This substitute is not by any means
> so glaringly inappropriate as the one he has chosen himself
> during symptom formation and yet sufficiently remote from
> the real source of anxiety to assist in fixing changes that have
> in any case been considerably reduced by other and more
> accurate analytic work. [p. 400]

Glover reasons that some inexact interpretations may
thus result in symptomatic improvement, but at the cost of

"refractoriness to deeper analysis" (p. 400). He concludes by saying: "The moral is of course that, unless one is sure of one's ground it is better to remain silent" (p. 400).

Of special interest in the Glover paper is his recognition that the interpretive scene is complex and often puzzling. Although he drew conclusions based on traditional psychoanalytic logic, he nonetheless helped to open the door to major reconsideration of the nature of interpretive action. Glover, however, does not recognize interpretation as an intersubjective human event; the interpersonal origins and effects are disregarded in favor of a purely intrapsychic consideration. And he concludes that one is morally obliged to remain silent in the face of uncertainty. Precisely the opposite is my recommendation: We should welcome uncertainty, interpret with foreknowledge of erring, and expect creative stimulation from the interpretation.

Strachey (1934) continued the evolving theory of interpretation with his explanation of how interpretations become "mutative interpretations." He attributes this result to very specific changes effected in the patient's superego through particular interpretive measures arising from the analyst's transference position. Strachey also acknowledges the presence of other powerful therapeutic influences by the analyst, but he excludes them from the category of interpretation.

Similar to Glover's interests some twenty-six years earlier, Loewenstein (1957) published some definitive ideas about interpretation in psychoanalysis during the heyday of ego psychology. The importance of the working alliance, the personalized relationship of analysand and analyst, and the identificatory and object-relational in the total interpretive situation are all subordinated by Loewenstein to the overriding issue of the "validation" of the interpretation and its consequent effectiveness in the deepening of insight. Loewenstein emphasizes, however, that accuracy alone does not fully determine an interpretation's effectiveness. "Preparation," "confrontation," and "clarification" are necessary precursors of interpretation. "Dosage, hierarchy, timing, and the wording" are also crucial to the total effect of interpretations. When Loewenstein addresses the question of how an analyst formulates interpretations, he attributes to the analyst an "intuitive grasping" of "preconscious clues" from the patient. Instead of exploring this experience of "intuitive grasping," he describes how the analyst's provisional hunches are verbalized and then modified and corrected by the analysand's reactions.

Loewenstein reveals a germinal appreciation of the creative ambiguities of interpretation by his reference to the "complex effects" of interpretations. He says these effects arise because interpretations often address wide "defensive structures" in the patient. He also calls upon Hartmann's (1951) notion of the "multiple appeal" of interpretations: "Although our interpretations deal directly and explicitly with only some of the facets and aspects of the conflict involved, they implicitly encompass and indirectly affect a much larger number of them" (p. 140). In the same vein, he notes Kris's (1951) contention that interpretive communications in psychoanalysis are never wholly "regulated" by the secondary process. They stimulate primary process reactions which, by definition, exercise their influence more inexactly and indirectly.

Hartmann, Loewenstein, and Kris stand directly athwart the path of exactitude exalted by Glover. These authors reveal a gradually increasing sensitivity to the inevitability of ambiguity, complexity, and unpredictability in the interpreting process, but they seem content to confine their explanations within the existing theoretical limits of their time. However, a richer understanding of psychoanalytic technique in general, and of interpretation in particular, was growing. Ego psychology, directly and indirectly, exposed the serious limitations of prior instinctually based explanations of the psychoanalytic process. It was becoming more evident that intrapsychic theories required interpersonal and intersubjective additions and emendations.

Especially vexing was the severely limited understanding of the importance of the human context so crucial to psychoanalysis, and so often ignored in the dynamic explanatory assertions. Concepts like Zetzel's (1956) "working alliance" and Greenson's (1965) "therapeutic alliance" were posited as sine qua nons for the therapeutic process. They had transferential, countertransferential, and reality characteristics, but they did not belong entirely in any of these categories. These concepts exemplified a theory of interpretation and cure in transition. They were like somewhat ungainly grafts on the trunk of psychoanalytic theory. Perhaps the most powerful effect of these concepts was their demand that the therapist be consciously and conceptually attuned to the specific person in the patient role. The emphasis on individualization helped stimulate reconsideration of the ways interpretations work, and even of the ways interpretations are formed. Knowingly or unknowingly, the way was being prepared for drastic reformulations of the entire field.

Perhaps the critical focus should now be on a theory of the *implicit* in which crucial ideas, values, feelings, and premises are, so to speak, packed between the lines or beneath the surface of an interpretation. From this perspective, a kind of reversal of importance occurs: The spoken words mediate and are subordinate; the unspoken words—the implicit—are the essence. The process itself, then, potentially discloses idea, value, feeling, premise.

While the assigned roles of patient and therapist influence the process at all levels from the outset, it is also true that to some extent the basic relatedness of therapist and patient has relatively little to do with their assigned roles in the treatment. In the second stage of interpretation the formal role assignment of the therapist is clearly dominant, enabling him or her to achieve the discipline acquired through training and experience that is necessary for the construction of the manifest interpretation.

In my view, an important aspect of an interpretation occurs outside the sphere of role assignment, formality, and discipline. The lineage of this notion extends back to Freud's (1912) references to the use of the analyst's unconscious as a receiving instrument, and in his advice to the analyst to follow his own associations, while listening to the patient's. He recognized the importance of the unconscious communication between analyst and patient, even while he attempted and failed to make psychoanalysis into an objective science. The elemental psychoanalytic events are utterly subjective, and must live and flourish free of the fetters of attempted objectification. This is demonstrated persuasively in the recent work of Jacobs (1985).

In 1985, relying in part on the work of Isakower (1957–1963), Jacobs pursued the subject of the unconscious communication occurring reciprocally in psychoanalysis:

> What was not discussed in Isakower's initial remarks was the way that the analytic instrument operates to promote and regulate the metacommunications between patient and analyst. That this kind of communication exists as an important aspect of every analytic hour is a well-known, if infrequently studied, phenomenon. Close scrutiny of the verbal exchanges that occur within a given analytic hour will reveal not only overt messages conveyed by both participants, but covert messages as well. The manifest content of the communication is accompanied by a latent content that comments, adds to, or modifies the manifest level. When his part of the analytic instrument is working well, the analyst will register with sensitivity the metacommunicative as well as the denotative aspects of the patient's communications. And his interventions will contain a latent message that reverberates with and responds to the latent messages inherent in the patient's verbalizations. [p. 56]

He continues:

> There is little doubt that this kind of message, the metacom-
> municative one, plays a significant role in every therapy. As
> yet its place in theory and technique has not been fully elu-
> cidated. But there is very little question that every correct
> interpretation is correct on more than one level. Grasping the
> essence of what the patient is attempting to convey, the an-
> alyst responds with a verbal interpretation indicating that he
> understands the message. But through his inflection, his tone,
> his timing, his phrasing, and particularly through the affect
> that he conveys, the analyst responds to another message, to
> the covert communication which, often enough, contains
> within it a comment on the interaction between patient and
> analyst. When the analytic instrument is operating on only
> one channel and fails to register the patient's metacommun-
> ications, the analyst's "correct" interpretation may elicit little
> response because it is, in fact, only partially correct. But when
> the analytic instrument is well tuned and is able to register
> on several channels at once, the analyst's intervention will
> reflect his intuitive grasp of the multiple levels of meaning
> of the patient's communications. It is then that the patient
> has the experience of feeling truly understood. And it is at
> such times that his response to the analyst's interpretation
> will, in all likelihood, contain the confirming affects and as-
> sociations that have come to be associated with its correctness.
> [p. 57]

In a related paper that appeared a few years earlier, Balter
and colleagues (1980) also employ the concept of the
analyzing instrument. The analyzing instrument functions
when a special psychological linkage occurs between analyst
and analysand. These authors postulate three preconditions
for the required state of mind in the analyst: "(1) the concentration of attention upon the analysand's communications; (2) the concentration of attention upon the analyst's
own internal perceptions; and (3) the suspension of critical

activity regarding these two objects of the analyst's attention" (p. 485). They go on to state that the similar preconditions in both analyst and analysand

> . . . induce a situation-specific and goal-specific regressed state of mind in each. We have termed the state of mind a subsystem in the ego of each participant. The analyzing instrument in operation consists of the two subsystems functioning together. The content evoked in each subsystem derives from the fantasy-memory constellations of each participant in response to the communications from the other. The ultimate result is the elucidation of the fantasy-memory constellations of the analysand. [p. 502]

The notion of an analyzing instrument has been valuable in directing attention to the obscure but powerful impact of the unconscious interplay of patient and therapist. Its disadvantage arises from the reifying implication inhering in the concept. After all, the term "instrument" strongly connotes mechanical, technical structure and function, quite unsuitable for mediation and explanation of the unconscious transactions of psychotherapy, with all their mystery and intimacy. The notion has now become an archaic artifact, overtaken by other important developments in psychotherapy, such as the concept of intersubjectivity.

By way of contrast, it should also be noted that neither Jacobs (1985) nor Balter and colleagues (1980) have taken the decisive step of attributing a primary initiating role to the therapist's unconscious life in the creation of the treatment situation, a role in some ways coequal to that of the patient.

The term *intersubjectivity* emerged from the existential literature in the mid-1970s. Trevarthan (1980) then employed the concept in theorizing about observations of infant–mother developmental transactions. These contributions obviously converged with the attention to experience-nearness being given by a new group of psychoanalytic theorists. The most cohesive and explicit exponents of drastically revised psychoanalytic theory and practice were Heinz Kohut (1977) and his followers, who called themselves self psychologists. The term *experience-nearness* emphasizes the subjective involvement of the therapist and epitomizes this movement, which eschews the ideal of a detached, aloof, and objective therapist. This latter stance, the self psychologists feel, is derived from a false theory and inevitably leads to false interventions.

In their efforts to develop a more effective and valid theory of therapeutic action, Stolorow and his associates have brought out of the original Kohutian matrix the concept of intersubjectivity and presented it to a wide audience of psychotherapists. Ulman and Stolorow (1985) have stated, "We advance the proposition that transference and countertransference in their mutual interaction codetermine a specific intersubjective field of 'transference-countertransference neurosis.' This concept illuminates the unfolding of patients' and therapists' developmentally arrested structures . . ." (p. 37). They also state that "from an intersubjective viewpoint . . . both the transference and the countertransference continually shape one another in a specific pattern of reciprocal mutual influence" (p. 50). Also, "We believe this consistent focus on the interplay between the patient's and the therapist's developmentally arrested psychological structures was crucial for the unfolding of the therapeutic process" (p. 51).

This view is very similar to the fundamental proposition of the present work. At first reading it may appear virtually identical, but there are significant differences. In defining "transference-countertransference neurosis," they limit its meaning to ". . . the patient's and therapist's developmentally arrested psychological structures," and their case material supports this rendition.

However, Stolorow and Atwood (1984) also state: "The concept of transference may be understood to refer to all the ways in which the patient's experience of the analytic relationship becomes organized according to the configurations of self and object that unconsciously structure his subjective experience" (p. 47). They continue, "Countertransference, in turn, refers to how the structures of the analyst's subjectivity shape his experience of the analytic relationship and, in particular, of the patient's transference" (p. 47).

These last statements may be read to include the notion of the therapist's inner life having a *continuous* shaping influence on the analytic process. This reading is congruent with the point of view expressed earlier by Stolorow and Atwood (1979), in which they correlate the theoretical positions of various psychoanalytic thinkers with the crucial issues of their respective individual lives.

Yet in all the case material published by Stolorow and his various associates, the clinical discussions invariably revolve around critical problematic moments or periods in the therapy and how these problems were resolved through the intersubjective analysis of the situation. They do not address the matter of the therapist's subjective input before the crisis or impasse occurred or after it was resolved. The emphasis regularly is on the reactivity of the therapist, rather than on his or her initiating influence.

Stolorow and Atwood (1984), for example, state: "the configurations of self and object structuring the patient's experience give rise to expressions that are assimilated into closely similar central configurations in the psychological life of the analyst" (p. 47). Their formulation suggests that the patient acts and the analyst reacts in this conceptual discussion of intersubjective conjunction. Again, they add that intersubjective disjunction "occurs when the analyst assimilates the material expressed by the patient into configurations that significantly alter its subjective meaning for the patient" (p. 47). The emphasis thus remains on the analyst's receptiveness or lack thereof.

These authors recommend "reflective self awareness"

as involving a capacity in the therapist to decenter from his or her subjective world, which enables empathic understanding to develop, and only when this capability exists can either subjective conjunction or disjunction be productively utilized. Once more, only the patient's activity initiates the intersubjective process, so that the initiating processes appear to be unidirectional. No reference can be found indicating that unconscious self-initiated stimuli from the therapist constantly impinge upon the analysand, thus creating coequality in the production of the basic emotional conditions of the therapist.

I believe that Stolorow and associates (1987) conflate countertransference and intersubjectivity, limiting their interest in intersubjectivity to the pathological aspects of the therapist's reciprocal interaction with the analysand. They implicitly disregard the intercritical periods of the therapy, during which the singular unconscious life of the therapist continues to be a significant influence on the treatment, even if no countertransference complication has arisen.

The work of Stolorow and associates remains important. However, if we are to arrive at a theory of interpretation, we must establish as clearly as possible what their work says and what it does not say regarding the fundamental process of interpretation formation. A low level of positivism seeps into their position. They present the therapist as initially relatively relaxed and neutral, unlike the patient, whose subjective turbulence activates the therapist's relevant subjective potentials, resulting in a conjunctive or disjunctive response. The therapist reflects on this, gains empathic power, and intervenes effectively. Then the therapist's idiosyncratic subjectivity apparently recedes into a state of benign receptiveness until the next impingement from the patient occurs, starting the same cycle once again.

The contributions of Schafer (1983), Gill (1982), and Levenson (1983), although formulated with less precision, foster the possibility of a more complete intersubjective explanation of interpretation. If the nonpathological aspects of the therapist's unconscious life are either omitted or excluded from consideration as contributing to the therapeutic process, the theorist inevitably pathologizes the process and thus in effect endorses the traditionally assumed view that during intercritical, non-neurotic periods of analytic activity, the unconscious life of the therapist does not help shape the therapeutic process. Actually, the therapist's unconscious contributions are continuous and always relevant to the therapeutic process. Thus the term *transference–countertransference,* unless clearly redefined to include all psychological events within each party and between both parties, is not a satisfactory overarching term and is insufficient to explain the full intersubjective meaning of interpretation. Nothing short of a complete inclusion of all psychological input and reactions of both participants will permit optimal understanding of the issue.

In the first stage of interpretation, healthy and sick structures in the two parties need not be distinguished. This permits the ever-active fantasy life of the analyst to shape as well as be shaped continuously in the intersubjective matrix. The distinction between healthy and unhealthy fantasies of the therapist applies essentially to the second stage of interpretive action, when education and professional experience, involving the therapist's professional ego identity, do become a factor.

During the second stage, complex choices are made that determine the therapist's interventions and whether these are productive or destructive. Thus, the basic emotional contributions and reactions of the therapist, that is, those of the first stage, are neither sick nor healthy. An illustration of this point is made in Winnicott's (1965) elucidation of the constructive role of hate in the countertransference. But this hatred is not always utilized productively; the same hatred can destroy a therapy. The crucial determinants here are how the analyst deals with his or her basic desires, urges, fantasies.

This in turn depends upon how effective the therapist's own treatment has been and, consequently, upon the skillful and sensitive, or maladroit and insensitive, functioning of his or her professional work ego. The therapist's fundamental passions in continuous reciprocal engagement with the patient's can, and do, depending upon the therapist's insight and professional skill (second stage functions), form the basis for productive interactions or destructive acting out.

Other recent work supports this view of the psychoanalytic process. Stern (1985) has offered a sensitive and detailed developmental study of mother–child transactions. Intersubjectivity is a crucial concept for his explanations of how mother and child develop within their intimate and reciprocally influential relationship. While he warns against indiscriminate equating of mother–infant intersubjectivity and therapist–patient intersubjectivity, much therapeutic illumination can be obtained from his studies of mother–infant transactions.

Stern cites the work of Shields (1978), Newson (1977), Vygotsky (1962, 1966), and others who, from the time of the infant's birth, in Stern's view, are in agreement that

> . . . (the mother) interprets all the infant's behaviors in terms of meanings; that is, she attributes meanings to them. She provides the semantic element, all by herself at first, and continues to bring the infant's behavior into her framework of created meanings. Gradually, as the infant is able, the framework of meaning becomes mutually created. This approach, based on social experience, might be called the approach of interpersonal meanings.

Many thinkers in France and Switzerland have independently approached the problem along similar lines and pushed the notion of maternal interpretation into richer clinical territory. They assert that mother's "meanings" reflect not only what she observes but also her fantasies about who the infant is and is to become. Intersubjectivity, for them, ultimately involves interfantasy. They have asked how the fantasies of the parent come to influence the infant's behavior and ultimately to shape the infant's own fantasies. This reciprocal fantasy interaction is a form of created interpersonal meaning at the covert level. . . . The creation of such meanings has been called "interactions fantasmatique." [p. 123]

These comments from students of infant development are extremely useful in the reformulation of the intersubjective theory of interpretation that is being offered here. A most important lesson for psychoanalysis and psychoanalytic psychotherapy is that interpretation, interpersonal meaning, and reciprocal fantasy interaction are interdependent concepts, of fundamental human importance, and continuously present. These views firmly support the need for elaboration and clarification of intersubjective processes in psychoanalysis and psychotherapy. The consideration of these processes must not be limited to examples of pathological intersubjective events. Such limitation simultaneously pathologizes and neutralizes intersubjectivity, inadvertently re-creating the traditional therapist–patient dichotomy and weakening the integrity of the concept of intersubjectivity.

Progress in the understanding of psychoanalytic interpretation requires that eponymous connotations of the term *interpretation* be further eroded. It is no longer appropriate for analytically oriented therapists to worry whether they are adhering scrupulously to the specifics or generalities of interpretation set forth in Freud (1900). Freud (1911) had a complex and subtle understanding of psychotherapeutic process, including interpretation, but the scientistic tendencies in his work frequently obstruct more complete and free access to latent meanings. Stern's work does not set out to invalidate Freud's (1910b) conflict theory. In fact, infant development studies may eventually support and enrich it. But this new work does dethrone and desanctify Freud's pronouncements, thereby endowing them with a new and stimulating ambiguity, which in turn revitalizes concept formation in psychoanalysis and psychotherapy.

When Rycroft (1985) urged therapists to treat psychoanalytic theory as a quarry, rather than as an edifice, he offered a creative alternative to the extremes of a slavish devotion to Freud or an iconoclastic repudiation of Freud. His was essentially a plea for open-mindedness, ambiguity, and exploration. He was attempting to find a way to incorporate new experiences and ideas with the old.

Schafer (1983) and Levenson (1983) also adhere to open-mindedness, ambiguity, and exploration in psychoanalytic interpretations. They strive for understanding and progressive change. Schafer comes from within the Freudian orientation; Levenson is non-Freudian, an interpersonalist. Schafer's Freudian orientation and Levenson's non-Freudian orientation are evident in the primacy of Freud's thinking— or the absence of the same—in each author's writings. Schafer is Freudian because he bases his contributions on Freud's work. On the other hand, although Levenson deeply respects Freud's ideas, he does not have a primary and central regard for them. In effect, he thinks of Freud as coequal with various other important psychoanalytic thinkers.

In his major work, *The Analytic Attitude,* Schafer (1983) covers the entire psychoanalytic spectrum. The title itself suggests an implicit intersubjective approach, rather than the traditional objectifying effort. An attitude is invariably a complex subjective state of being deriving from multiple experiential factors. The attribution of an attitude to the analyst, and its exhaustive investigation, certainly implies that Schafer perceives the analyst's subjective involvement in the analysis as supremely important. Schafer believes interpretations are the analyst's highly personal expressions; they are creative narrations, expressing the intersubjective character of making interpretations:

> I focus not so much on the content of interpretation of the sort one finds in text books that deal narrowly with technique or with specific theories of psychical development or psychopathology; much more, I focus on the presuppositions of making any interpretations at all, the structure and logical justification of interpretation, the ways in which interpretation is a form of narration through creating life histories and treatment histories, and the ways in which it is circular and self-confirming but not on that account foolish, false, or unhelpful. Much neglected by analytic theorists and teachers of technique, the theory of interpretation makes clear just what kind of work one does in doing analysis. So long as the theory of interpretation continues to be neglected, our understanding of the major cognitive aspect of the analytic attitude will remain in a primitive state, and the further result will be the needless controversy, dogmatism, and self-misunderstanding that in my view, characterize a good deal of psychoanalytic discussion. [p. ix]

Repeatedly, Schafer's comments on interpretation hover and circle around the intersubjective field, without explicitly entering it. This is shown in his discussion of the interpretation of transference and the conditions of loving: "In the psychology of metaphor we shall find a useful analogy to the psychology of transference interpretations" (p. 127).

> Some literary and linguistic analysts . . . believe that there are experiences that can only be expressed metaphorically. [p. 127]

> It seems justified to conclude that the metaphor is a new experience rather than a mere paraphrase of an already fully constituted experience. The metaphor creates an experience that one has never had before. [p. 127]

It is a creation rather than a mere paraphrase. . . . [p. 128]

In steadfastly and perspicaciously making transference interpretations, the analyst helps constitute new modes of experience and new experiences. [p. 130]

Interpretation is a creative redescription. [p. 130, Schafer's italics]

It is wrong to think that interpretation deals only with what is concealed or disguised or, what is its correlate, that "the unconscious" is omniscient. In particular, it cannot be the case [that] "the unconscious" knows all about transference and repetition. [p. 133]

Schafer also notes: "The process of interpretation does not conform to the official and traditional epistemological model of psychoanalysis, that is, the model of positivism . . . to the contrary . . . there can be no sharp split between observer and observed or between subject and object . . ." (p. 188). He adds that psychoanalytic interpretations are worked out in an "inevitable circular, nonpositivistic and collaborative manner" (p. 189). In this spirit, Schafer also says: "Interpretation is more than uncovering; it is discovering, transforming, or creating meaning, too" (p. 87).

Schafer describes the factors that "facilitate the analyst's relatively secure and complex empathizing at work. . ." (p. 38). These include:

1. having less at stake than the analysand;

2. knowing so much about the analysand's intimate life (apparently in contrast to the analysand's scant knowledge about the analyst);

3. not being constrained to respond overtly (also unlike the analysand);

4. being primarily responsible to formulate appropriate interpretations;

5. benefitting from a "work ego" and a "work superego" (derived from training and professional identification);

6. enjoying benefits of familiarity with his or her own unconscious tendencies and defenses through personal analysis and supervision;

7. knowing that the analytic closeness will diminish with termination.

This profile of the "informed, disinterested, and empathic analyst is not an idealization," but an "ideal form with reference to which one may hope to explain the often observed discrepancy . . . between the competent analyst's analytic and nonanalytic relationships" (pp. 38–39).

The factors mentioned include some that clearly are functions assigned to the second stage of interpretation in this book—the ones that are direct and indirect results of the analytic training, such as availability of technical resources, the analytic "work ego," and the benefits of identifications with important teachers. Other factors cited by Schafer seem to suggest a fundamentally attenuated subjectivity of the analytic therapist. This, I believe, results from Schafer's erroneous conflation of the two stages of analytic interpretation.

Elsewhere, Schafer (1985) refers to intersubjectivity. I believe he blurs its meaning by implying that it exists in antithetical relationship to interpretation and insight. He seems to suggest that an analytic stance is either more reflective and interpretive or more interactive and intersubjective. He prefers a blend of these allegedly opposing qualities. Intersubjectivity should not be equated with specific behaviors by the therapist, such as talkativeness, nor should it be viewed as antagonistic to interpretation. In fact, intersubjectivity is indispensable to interpretation, since it is the intersubjective process that lays the foundation for the first stage of interpretation.

Apparently Schafer does not accept a basically coequal emotional involvement by analysand and analyst, and does not recognize or acknowledge a first, precognitive, passionate experience between the two people. It is through the experience of this "primitive" first stage that the analyst of the second stage, intuitive and insightful, becomes possible. Otherwise, the analyst's experiential immersion is shallow, and the transformational potential of his or her interpretations is correspondingly reduced.

In effect, Schafer appears to be proposing that the analyst is, and is not, subjectively committed to the analysis. This seems to constitute a contemporary restatement of Freud's contradictory advice that the analyst use his or her unconscious like a receiving instrument and at the same time be a blank screen.

Schafer's discussions are richly textured and deliberately ambiguous. It is difficult to ascertain with confidence whether he believes, or does not believe, that the analyst makes a continuous, idiosyncratic, subjective contribution to the psychoanalytic experience. He notes the bilateral contribution to the narrative structure of a psychoanalysis, and emphasizes the collaborative creativity of analyst and analysand. These assertions indicate a potential belief in an intersubjective fundament to the psychoanalytic situation.

Levenson (1983) values the interpersonal and the ambiguous. He perceives psychoanalytic progress as characterized by an enlarged consciousness, which is rich and supple, and not a purer, clarified consciousness. The latter is an explicit Freudian perspective that Levenson attacks on the basis of reductionism. This is somewhat simplistic and unfair because most Freudians are fully aware of the hazards of reductionism. However, reductionist tendencies do inhere in Freudian theory, and it is useful to reconsider their pitfalls.

Levenson explicitly, and with admirable consistency, eschews any reductionist inclinations. While he does not specifically include the term *intersubjectivity* in his reflections, his thinking about the analytic process is largely compatible with an intersubjective approach. The dedication to ambiguity affiliates Levenson closely with the intersubjective. He carefully demolishes any pretensions of the analyst to special status, power, or role. So from the outset, a state of benign, creative disorder is striven for. The avoidance of any belief in a preordination of events establishes the possibility that the powerful unconscious tendencies of both parties are more likely to become evident and accessible than if a more ordered kind of role assignment were assumed. It seems correct that classical psychoanalysis presupposes at least a more definitive separation of roles of analyst and analysand—both conceptual and behavioral—than does the interpersonal psychoanalytic model.

Levenson (1983), in *The Ambiguity of Change,* consistently debunks the unique wisdom of the analyst. He states:

> The thesis, then, is that psychoanalysis works not because of what it says but how it proceeds, throwing an ever-widening seine of inquiry that is of a semiotic nature. The uniqueness of psychoanalysis lies in its particular framing, which permits the participants to use themselves in an infinite regress of metacommunication about the data the patient presents about his or her life. The therapist's particular explanatory system is only a metaphor, a way of pulling things together, of parenthesizing data. It is neither intrinsically correct nor incorrect but, rather, a commentary on the interactional field. But since each commentary is a selection of position, however inadvertent an attitude about what is being told by the patient, every interpretation becomes an interaction. [p. 111]

Repeatedly, Levenson describes the complexities of the analytic situation, which render efforts at clarification misleading and futile:

> The therapist does not explain content, he expands awareness of patterning. [p. 116]

Insight would be not seen so much as accreted learning but as a more holistic, total reorganization of the "reality within." All the parameters will change simultaneously and totally and really without a rational or logical framework of explanation. The hermeneutics may be an epiphenomenon, merely a codicil to change. [p. 117]

Even closer to the intersubjective viewpoint, Levenson avers:

The therapist becomes part of the problem to resolve it. [p. 117]

Interpreting or explaining superimposes a linear explanation on a complex, undelineated analogic activity. It brackets and forces one aspect or perspective on an interpersonal field that is, if one extends it into the social matrix, infinite. Explanation says, "Look here, settle for this aspect. It is reductive, delineating" (p. 117). Finally, "Why should the analyst know what is wrong with the patient? Clever analysts have always known that their function is paradoxical. It is the goal of the therapist to fail the patient's expectations, not to meet them." [p. 121]

But here Levenson may be committing a categorical error by making interpretation synonymous with explanation, thereby abolishing the crucial distinction between the positivistic essence of explanation and the intersubjective possibility of interpretation. Elsewhere, Levenson asks:

Can one label it countertransference if the therapist has never disliked this man who is unfailingly attractive, intelligent, and decent? Is it worth noting that he never makes the therapist feel stupid, unpleasant, or unlikable? Is it countertransference if one doesn't have a countertransference? Perhaps the key to therapy is for the therapist to experience the patient in some real way, even if with contempt, disdain or total boredom. [p. 46]

Levenson apparently regards the possibilities of error by the analyst, due to unconscious countertransference, to be both inevitable and (if properly dealt with) therapeutically valuable. He notes: "Participant-observation should not be delegated to the therapist. It is a mutual effort. Catching the therapist in a self-serving operation may do more for the patient's sense of competence than a lifetime of benevolent participations" (p. 157). Such observations by Levenson demonstrate an appreciation of the intersubjective nature of psychoanalytic events. The commentary, perhaps deliberately, does not commit the analyst to a passionate coequality with the analysand. Nevertheless, Levenson's position seems compatible with such an assumption.

Levenson is a freewheeling, intellectual interpersonalist, whereas Schafer emerges as a cautious, reflective Freudian revisionist. Perhaps a fringe benefit of the juxtaposition of these contrasting thinkers, with their similar views of the analytic process, is the demonstration that the ardent search for meaning reduces the tendentious power of theoretical predisposition. Schafer and Levenson share a certain vagueness about the problem of the essential, initiating, coequal role of the analyst in the analytic process. Probably, the radical implications of a relentless intersubjective analysis are as yet unacceptable to both theorists, although their work contributes to an intersubjective mode of thought about analytic interactions. These thoughts of course apply to dynamic psychotherapy in general, not only to psychoanalysis.

The clinically experienced reader of Schafer and Levenson discovers a powerful commonality in their work: the sophisticated exploration of the seemingly boundless complexity of the psychotherapeutic situation. The common effect upon the reader is a textural enrichment of his or her psychotherapeutic consciousness. Preexisting concepts become less clear and cannot be so firmly held. Inexorably, these changes prepare the way for transforming ways of conceiving (or reconceiving) the psychotherapeutic process.

Further solid support for an intersubjective theory of interpretation is provided by Gill (1982), who has employed careful clinical study to demonstrate the interpersonal and creative elements in transference, in addition to its usual intrapsychic and replicative features. Gill's (1982) work emphasizes that analysts have not understood transference and therefore have not analyzed it with sufficient consistency and skill. But he redefines transference so that it is no longer "a distortion of the present by the past"; instead, it is "always an amalgam of past and present" (p. 177). He therefore decides "that the analyst is perforce a participant–observer (Sullivan's term) rather than merely an observer," and that "the transference is a resultant of the interaction between the patient and the analyst . . ." (p. 177).

Gill believes that analysts, including Freud, have not analyzed transference thoroughly enough and have not recognized the role of the realistic relationship between analyst and analysand in the shaping of the whole analysis, including the transference. He contends that unlike Freud, subsequent analysts have tried to purify analysis by excluding the real relationship and becoming overly preoccupied with technique. They have paradoxically vitiated their own efforts by a desiccating misunderstanding of the transference. Gill writes: ". . . [A] major trend in current practice is to expunge the personal relationship instead of recognizing it as part of the inevitably existing actuality of the analytic situation. . . . The belief that something was amiss led to the concepts of the alliances and efforts to promote them . . . as technical precepts" (p. 141). Gill contends that analysts err seriously in isolating technique from the person of the analyst and the actual situation.

Gill's contribution to psychotherapeutic thinking is his recognition of the uniqueness of each therapeutic relationship. He insists that the singular characteristics of the analyst, as well as of the analysand, create the unique situation that must be included in the process of analytic understanding, rather than be subjected to some artificial and unsuccessful effort at exclusion by a rigid technique. He does not, however, appear to accord explicitly to the analyst's unconscious the degree of influence permitted by the intersubjective point of view. Yet his work clearly encourages psychotherapists to appreciate the importance of their personal, subjective participation in the therapeutic process.

Another source of support for the intersubjective origins of interpretations comes from current literary criticism of psychoanalysis. Janet Malcolm (1987) cites several critics who give examples in Freud's writings of the contribution of Freud's (1905) fantasy life to his interpretations. She notes Jane Gallop's contention that Freud's interpretations to Dora were "titillating, coy, flirtatious." She bases this on Freud's claim that he was behaving quite differently but gave himself away by his use of the ambiguous French aphorism, *J'appelle un chat un chat* (p. 87). Malcolm quotes Toril Moi, who similarly believes that Freud's interpretations of a fellatio fantasy in Dora arose as follows: "It is more than probable that the fantsay was not in Dora's mind, but in his (Freud's) alone" (p. 88). Malcolm further cites another Dora scholar, Neil Hertz, who makes a similar point.

Malcolm's analysis attributes transferential contributions to the interpretation and reinterpretation of fellatio fantasies by all of the involved parties. Dora had an erotic transference to Freud; Freud had an erotic transference (or countertransference) to Dora, while Gallop, Moi, and Hertz seem to have their own erotic transferences to the master. Malcolm does not mention her own subjective involvement.

The importance of these examinations of psychoanalytic

interpretations resides in their exegetical discoveries of the complex set of interacting meanings and motives that become distilled in the interpretation. In this sense, an interpretation can be regarded as a highly condensed statement of the powerful interplay of human needs in a particular psychosocial context: the psychoanalytic situation. Interpretation traditionally was conceived analogically, like a medication given to the patient in a certain dosage and via a certain route, or like a careful surgical intervention. As Gill (1982) emphasizes in his criticism of the search for pure technique, this covert definition of interpretation, and of the psychotherapeutic process, can no longer be seriously entertained.

Interpretation no longer possesses the precision and convenience of definition gained through analogy and a positivist orientation, but it has been enormously enriched by the inclusion of the intersubjective and interpersonal perspectives. In a sense, the importance of interpretation was undervalued in the past when it was essentially conceived as a technical device. The new understanding makes interpretation available as a process, as an important aspect of the analytic experience, as an expression of and a contribution to the underlying and ever-present human relationship.

Beginning with Freud (1900), interpretation has been actually perceived as a more complex phenomenon than has formally been acknowledged. The complexity has derived primarily from the role of the therapist's unconscious in the production of interpretation. Thinkers, including Freud, have regularly issued clearly defined versions of the nature of psychotherapeutic interventions that have been at variance with one another. Freud (1912) has made contradictory assertions regarding the analyst's unconscious contributions to the analytic process. He offered the concept of countertransference, which indicated that neurotic problems generated unconscious input by the analyst. But he did not clearly define the similarities or differences between countertransference and the unconscious activity of the analyst, which he realized helped establish the therapeutically desirable unconscious communication of analyst and analysand. Probably the traditional psychoanalytic response would be that there are two different types of unconscious activity, but as countertransference has gradually lost its essentially pathogenic meaning, this customary distinction becomes less and less tenable.

A more timely recognition of the ever-present subjective influence by the analyst on the analytic process would have precluded the possibility of simplistic and deceptively attractive pronouncements about the clearly defined nature of various psychoanalytic phenomena. For instance, interpretation would have been defined more loosely, and the definition would have acknowledged the powerful contribution provided by the therapist's own subjective life. Although such recognition would have reduced the intrapsychic dominance in psychoanalytic theorizing, it would have been in greater conformity with clinical realities and would have promoted gradual, nonpolemical progress toward sound psychoanalytic theory and technique.

The concept of intersubjectivity has become a crucial component of psychodynamic thinking. It is both pointed and widely embracing, thus capturing and underlining the basically human nature of therapeutic transactions. It promotes realistic thinking about the therapist's role, and it reduces the seductive appeal of expedient efforts to objectify the therapeutic situation, efforts that are always simplistic in essence and misleading in effect.

7

CLINICAL CATEGORIES OF INTERPRETATION

Valid interpretations arise naturally, they express the intersubjective process, and they contribute to that same process. Conversely, statements artificially constructed and purported to be interpretations may disrupt the intersubjective process and are felt to be unempathic by the patient. Such pseudo-interpretations are disguised expressions of the inner fantasy activity of the therapist who resists the intersubjective process and is therefore out of touch with the patient's fantasy.

Interpretations that arise naturally flow from and into the psychotherapeutic dialogue. "Artificial" interpretations have a coercive quality with respect to the dialogue and are experienced by patients as violative. They elicit a specific, violent emotional response. If the general quality of the relationship is satisfactory, the patient will probably communicate these painful sentiments, and of course the therapist should listen very carefully, and should immediately look into himself for the inner source of the disruptive motive.

Stolorow and Atwood (1984) have described an "intersubjective disjunction" in which, for countertransferential reasons, the therapist is unable to be attuned to the patient. I believe this uncorrected circumstance also produces disruptive interpretations. If the therapist can hear the patient's pained response, it becomes possible for the therapist to scrutinize his or her interior life to identify the dissonant factors and reestablish empathic contact. When the psychotherapeutic relationship is already severely distorted and the therapist remains oblivious, the patient will not feel free to verbalize these important feelings. They will go underground, reinforcing impasse and leading to abrogation of the therapy.

Effective interpretations, that is, those that arise naturally, will achieve one or another of several forms that may be called classes or types of interpretations. The particular form taken by an interpretation is determined by the dominant emphasis in the current dialogue. I will outline the classes and give a series of detailed examples of how these interpretations arise and how they influence the therapeutic process.

The therapist usually is not, and probably usually should not be, clearly aware of the complex set of ideas, desires, and defenses going on within and between the two parties as an interpretation is being developed. The search for literal precision in our work seems inadvisable. Every interpretation is a creative act that emerges naturally from the creative interaction of patient and analyst. No two interpretations can be identical because no two moments of human experience are ever identical. Obviously, however, similarities do exist, and the detection of these similarities provides the basis for classifying interpretations.

Before proceeding to the classification and examples, another important aspect of making interpretations deserves mention. The analyst never knows whether an interpretation is correct, because the analyst can never (and optimally should never) possess in consciousness a complete comprehension of all the ingredients contributing to the situation. To wait expectantly, even passively, for this degree of certainty may seriously distort the therapeutic process. So the analyst makes a sophisticated guess, prepares for the high probability of error, and expects a flawed but constructive consequence of the interpretation. The element of flaw becomes the goad that encourages the recipient, and then the interpreter, to continue the expressive search. A flawed interpretation also provides the two parties with a measure of the degree to which they are separated in their intimate, intersubjective transaction. In effect, the flaw in the interpretation is one of its most important characteristics.

The following classification of interpretation is also flawed. The different types are not intended to designate precise characteristics. Nor do they represent utterly different kinds of interpretations. It is instead a matter of emphasis; the dominant intersubjective focus is the basis for the designation. I have previously suggested (Natterson 1986) a classification of interpretation, and I am essentially adhering to it here. The following is the classification:

1. Past–present interpretation

2. Intellectualized interpretation

3. Empathic interpretation

4. Transference interpretation

5. Interpretation linking therapeutic reality and transference

6. Interpretation of resistance

7. Affect-laden interpretation

The clinical case examples that follow will illustrate each of these types and their intersubjective characteristics.

PAST–PRESENT INTERPRETATION

This is interpretation as it is generally understood by the public. In this scenario, the patient visits a therapist to discuss symptoms and problems. The therapist then tells the patient what noxious childhood event or figure has caused the present difficulty, and the patient is cured. Of course, such a scenario is rare. This kind of psychologizing may have some very limited value, but it is formulaic as well as adynamic, and it is not a genuine interpretation.

Because interpretations are made in a psychotherapeutic context, attempts to interpret symptoms, affects, or behavior without regard for the therapeutic circumstances can be disruptive. Such efforts can divert attention from the underlying therapeutic process, thereby generating confusion instead of insight. Conversely, past–present interpretations can be quite valuable if the foregoing phenomena can be linked through the patient's associations to some crucial life issue. For example, an interpretation that relates a symptom to important historical circumstances may be powerfully effective. A past–present interpretation should be anchored in the immediate therapeutic encounter; otherwise it is disruptive and defensive. This type of interpretation implicitly includes the therapeutic relationship and thus increases the texture, breadth, and depth of the patient's awareness.

Why, then, may therapists not heed these requirements of an interpretive reference to the past? Often such neglect occurs because the therapist is unable to cope with the anxiety of intense encounter with the patient. The therapist, needing distance, is tempted to make a diversionary reference to a remote period of the patient's life and an inappropriate past–

present interpretation is offered. It is an ironic probability that if such a therapist had a more integrated understanding of his or her own past, disruptive comments about the patient's past would not occur.

If the therapist is reacting authentically and nondefensively to the patient's immediate therapeutic behavior, then a past–present interpretation will very likely be based upon an appropriate intersubjective response. For example, if the patient's comments have vital impact upon the therapist, and if the therapist experiences some emotion-laden memory of his or her own past, then an interpretation that relates an aspect of the patient's current life to some important childhood issue may well enrich, rather than deplete, the immediate therapeutic situation.

Therapy is much more natural, even easy, if the therapist's feelings and thoughts flow along with the patient's. This contrasts sharply with therapy in which the therapist attempts to maintain a cool, cognitive mastery, hoping thereby to understand objectively the intricacies of the patient's associations and to avoid an appraisal tainted with his or her own subjectivity.

Boundaries between people are best when they are open and unguarded and permit free movement from one side to the other. The same is true of the interface of therapist and patient. If either party is overconcerned with separateness, with avoidance of fusion or merger, or has an excessive need to merge, then the normal process of union and separation, separation and union, is seriously disturbed, and a corresponding interference with therapeutic action is created. The ensuing aloofness of the therapist may engender a disposition toward unfeeling past–present interpretation. By contrast, a fluent psychotherapeutic process may encourage interpretations of the past that are vital, fitting, and helpful.

Past–present interpretations help and satisfy those patients for whom the historical dimension is an active part of their conscious psychological lives. By contrast, patients who suffer from a kind of ahistoricity desperately need openings into the past, even though they tend to be refractory to such interpretations. If therapists work to overcome these resistances to the historical perspective, this sometimes leads to greater receptiveness. The case of C. M. illustrates the intersubjective underpinning of past–present interpretation. The patient and I often interacted around a shared axial issue of gastrointestinal symptoms. These symptoms in each of us involved interrelationships of self, mother, and siblings in childhood. Furthermore, our respective alimentary pasts blatantly colored therapeutic consciousness. These included fantasies of loving and being loved by mother, of being neglected by mother, of being mother to siblings, of being mothered by siblings. These and similar meanings were continuously, and often unconsciously, attributed and conveyed to one another. It was quite natural for past–present interpretations to be prominent in this analytic therapy.

C. M., a social worker, first consulted me because of generalized anxiety, phobic anxiety, and a threatening level of incompatibility in her relatively new marriage. Fear of vomiting in a closed moving vehicle, especially an airplane, constituted her main phobic concern.

C. M.'s family history was as follows: Her parents were successful, creative, liberal intellectuals. She, a younger sister, and a younger brother were all introspective high achievers.

C. M.'s marital life improved, and her general anxiety diminished markedly in the first year of analytic therapy. Initially, I had charged a very low fee. Her practice improved and I attempted to raise her fee after about one year. She used this occasion to break off therapy. Approximately one year later she resumed therapy, acknowledging the folly of her premature interruption but blaming me for permitting her to leave. She was now determined to eliminate her phobias and to prepare herself for motherhood.

Throughout therapy, the gastrointestinal issue loomed. C. M. had now developed severe, intermittent nausea, as well as a renewed fear of vomiting; these symptoms lasted for over two years, after which they disappeared as inexplicably as they had begun. During this period, she ran a gamut of doctors, each of whom regarded her symptoms as essentially of neurotic origin and who refused to give her ameliorative medications, as if they expected her to improve with their "explanation."

I felt C. M.'s anguish intensely because I too suffered from extended periods of gastrointestinal symptoms. I was able to accept her symptoms unconditionally; I did not impatiently expect their subsidence. I encouraged her to visit the physician whom I had eventually chosen to help me with my discomfort. She found his approach much more acceptable, and after another year, her symptoms largely subsided. No physiological cause was ever found.

C. M. had a family history of vomiting. Her mother not only vomited continually and neurotically, but she also conveyed strong messages of domestic and maternal incapability, particularly concerning food purchases and preparation. She was an obsessively worrying woman.

C. M.'s beloved grandfather, moreover, was an intimidating and frightening figure. After several years of therapy, as she was describing this clinically paranoid maternal grandfather, who always carried a gun, I told her that as a family legacy, she suffered with "intestinal paranoia." I further suggested that the dynamics of her maternal family had involved the transmission of high levels of anxiety and vigilance from one generation to another, resulting in the patient's own inability to relax.

My interpretation amused her and helped her recognize that her present surplus anxiety was due to conflicts engendered in the past. Interpretation linking past to present was the type most frequently employed with this patient. As she referred to her paranoid relative, I was aware of how my own gastrointestinal tension correlates with apprehension about environmental danger. This thought triggered my interpretation.

The seeming simplicity of the interpretation should not serve to conceal its subtextual complexity from the reader. The ease of formulation and reception resulted from a complex therapeutic process of many months' duration. The patient and I had developed a special mode of verbal and nonverbal communication that established certain interpretive norms for us. My comments on the psychological transactions became very direct. As so often happens in successfully unfolding psychotherapy, caution gradually changed to candor.

In a sense, each interpretation contains all the important parts of the psychotherapy in a very highly distilled form. Therefore, a valid analysis of an interpretation requires discussion of the various antecedent events that converge to become the subtext of the interpretation.

Our earlier transactions significantly influenced the impact of my remark that she suffered with "intestinal paranoia." Superficially, the interpretation seemed to be a terse statement delivered by an efficient clinician who gets right to the source of the problem. And in part this was true. In C. M.'s fantasy of being rescued, I assumed meaning for her that had two components. In one, she attributed to me a clinical tenacity and ruthlessness (a benign version of qualities of the maternal grandfather). In the second component, I possessed a readiness to endure the bother and mess that C. M.'s mother avoided.

Also, it was quite clear to me that she and I were like two crampy, neglected children. In childhood, she had traveled long distances with her younger siblings to join her parents, who were working in other parts of this country or Europe. During these trips she was the caretaker. In the transference, I would assume a counterpart caretaking of her as a tougher, more experienced older sibling. My own memories of being cared for by older sisters instead of my mother helped me realize that I was identifying with the patient and providing her with the needed maternal attitude through the older sibling role.

It seems likely that as we conjoined our respective mini-dramas, we created together a new, improved version of her family drama that may, in turn, have reduced her level of anxiety and thus also reduced her gastrointestinal discomfort. This was accomplished by my implicit transmission to her of the strong message that she could now believe that effective parental care would occur. Consequently, she could relinquish her hypervigilance and the associated psychophysiological reactions, and she could also relinquish the mothering attitudes to her family. Previously, C. M. had acted like a "little mother" to her younger siblings. She felt toward her parents an excessive sense of loyalty that included a significant component of protectiveness, as though she had to mother them also. But now she was changing, becoming less protectively involved with her siblings and parents.

Concomitantly, she developed an exaggerated individualism, including a transient embrace of reactionary politics, which seemed to be a manifestation of her efforts to abandon her traditional role. This was an amusing aspect of her effort to distinguish herself from her parents, whose politics were very progressive. All this was occurring as her love for her husband grew, plans to become pregnant became more definite and precise, and thoughts of divorce disappeared. Her prevailing drama, or fantasy, became more powerfully that of younger sibling than premature parent. And this change enabled her to resume more gratifying progress in her life journey.

My fantasy of being a caretaking sibling was important primarily because it constituted the consciously available aspect of our intersubjective engagement. Numerous powerful associations illuminating my childhood gastrointestinal problems emerged from this focus. Those symptoms, which continued into my adult life, kept me focused sympathetically and intensely upon her suffering, so that she perceived me as consistently able to absorb her symptoms and complaints. Perhaps she and another therapist would have developed another intersubjective bridge. My point is not that the specific fantasy interaction described here was essential for her treatment. Rather, the point is that an intersubjective linkage always occurs in psychotherapy. The effective therapist utilizes this intersubjective process to propel the therapy forward. And the more conscious this utilization, the more benefit accrues to the patient.

I remember wondering if her previous internists may have experienced some discomfiting visceral response to C. M. and her symptoms. Within just a few months, two different internists evaluated her gastrointestinal symptoms, discovered no organic problem, became convinced that the symptoms were psychological, and on that basis reassured her. However, because her symptoms did not abate, both doctors became angry with her. She experienced these reactions as profoundly frightening, and she fled. Their clumsy management of her difficulties perhaps ensued from their defensive efforts to deal with their unease by avoidant methods, an option unavailable to the effective analytic therapist.

In this instance, my behaviors were greatly influenced by my idiosyncratic reactions. I found C. M.'s personality and appearance appealing to my caretaking impulses, which are linked to my own wishes to be helped, soothed, and comforted. Her wide blue eyes, fair skin, and dark hair reminded me of my mother, as did her earnest and open manner of relating. My fantasy memories recalled my mother's seeming constant readiness to provide a warm embrace and comforting words to help me through the numerous stomachaches and earaches of early childhood. Of course, a much different perception of my mother unconsciously coexisted with this happy one.

It seemed perfectly natural for C. M. and me to talk about nausea, vomiting, cramps, and diarrhea. In fact, such conversations constituted a significant part of the ambient conditions facilitating the therapeutic process. Thus, the interpretation "you are suffering with intestinal paranoia" was exceedingly complex. It referred to her mother and grandfather in a conscious but implicit way. It indicated that I could perceive and accept her as a frightened little girl who, although she needed mothering, instead had to provide it, not only for her siblings but for her parents. It conveyed to her that I was another one of the kids, albeit an older one, and that as an older brother, I would now take care of her. It suggested that organ preoccupations can have enough power to cross the generation barrier if the associated anxiety is intense enough. It also indicated that the gastrointestinal vulnerability would change if she could relinquish the "little mother" role and permit herself to be mothered, in fantasy, by me. The interpretation lasted only a few seconds in utterance, but it required many, many months for its development. Although proffered cheerfully, almost kiddingly, it in fact had great power for me as well as for her. It arose from the self-knowledge that my gut relaxes when I feel safer in the world.

This example shows that past–present interpretations possess particular power and elegance when the patient's transferential availability enables the historical theme to be woven into the therapeutic fabric. Otherwise, the interpretation becomes an intellectualized reconstruction, which has a different influence on the therapeutic process and a different intersubjective basis.

INTELLECTUALIZED INTERPRETATIONS

The neophyte in psychoanalytic therapy learns that intellectualization is a defense. While this is a useful and difficult lesson to learn, it also carries the risk of becoming a rationalization for latent anti-intellectual trends, promoting a falsely dichotomous view of thought and emotion. Patients living with inner chaos can obtain much benefit from explanatory, intellectualized interpretations. Such interpretations provide the supportive psychological structure they desperately need.

Those patients who employ denial and manic defenses especially need interpretations that build a bridge between their conscious experience and their underlying thoughts and feelings. Although these interpretations arise ostensibly from the conscious speculations of the analyst, without associative support from the patient, they are nonetheless experienced as powerful and valid by both parties.

When the patient does not provide an optimal mixture of emotions and ideas, the therapist cannot construct the usual experience-near interpretations. Hence intellectualized interpretations, based on the therapist's understanding of the psychodynamics, are necessary. These patients are often very depressed and chaotic beneath a façade of energetic purposefulness. If they have developed a strong bond with the therapist, then such intellectualized interpreting may restore a measure of inner order and coherence, even though they consciously disbelieve the interpretations.

The following case demonstrates the intersubjective basis for intellectualized interpretation in the treatment of this type of patient.

> The patient was a depressed, middle-aged woman who came to see me for help in coping with the death, of leukemia, several years earlier, of her 20-year-old daughter and the abandonment shortly thereafter by her husband, whom she deeply loved. Although she was now beginning to recover from the death of her daughter, she was far less able to deal with the loss of her husband. The patient had two other adult children, a daughter and a son. The patient was charming and cheerful even as she painted a grim family portrait.

Her mother was depressed when the patient was born, possibly because she had not yet recovered from the death of her last child, an infant son. She had made several suicide attempts and was chronically ill. There were two older sisters, one of whom was also chronically depressed—so severely that she committed suicide several years before the patient began therapy with me.

This woman had undertaken therapy several years earlier with limited success. Immediately before beginning therapy with me, she had begun with still another experienced therapist whom she found excessively formal and unavailable. In contrast, she quickly established a positive relationship with me that relieved her and gave her hope.

Two factors contributed to the rapid development of strong rapport. First, when she initially telephoned me and told me of her discouragement with her more recent psychiatrist, I immediately inferred a need, and responded to her with warm, active interest during this call. Second, by chance she told one of her close friends that she had called me. This woman had been in treatment with me a number of years earlier when her daughter was also dying of leukemia. She informed this patient how helpful her therapy with me had been, thus reinforcing the patient's positive attitude.

Although bright and empathic, this woman was singularly unable to integrate fairly obvious interpretations. For instance, it seemed clear to me that because she had been designated the successor to her dead infant brother and was her father's favorite, she had been able to identify more strongly with her father than had been possible for her sister. It further seemed that this identification had saved her from her sister's severe depressions, which resulted from the sister's identification with the seriously ill mother. When I conveyed these ideas to her, it was quite difficult for her to accept them as valid, and she did not have any conscious feeling about the interpretations. She relied so heavily on the denial of her own despair that she needed to minimize the meaning of these matters. We worked on this stringent denial, but only after two years of therapy could she consciously begin to feel sorrow for the profoundly unhappy lives of her mother and her dead sister. This increased awareness of feelings for other family members correlated positively with more understanding of the crucial role of identifications in the various family members.

Early in the treatment, I began interpreting that she had introjected her mother's depression and that she was filled with rage and guilt in relation to the frustrating mother. I added that this led to depression in her. She listened and understood, but she assured me that this made no psychological sense to her. I persevered, and she continued to listen. Later, I extended the interpretation by saying that this profound, mother-linked depression constituted her basic problem, but that it coexisted with an extremely strong sexualized attachment to her father, which engendered guilt and anxiety but also enabled her to adopt some of his ebullience, in turn helping her to develop her peppy, denying surface. I said that these would have to be understood much better in order to liberate her true self. For clarity and emphasis, I presented this information to the patient in the following verbal diagram:

1. cheery, hypomanic, denying surface, covering

2. guilty, anxious, eroticized involvement with father, including identification, covering

3. pregenital rage, guilt, and symbiotic preoccupation with mother's depression, covering

4. patient's true self

For many months we argued over my interpretations, which I derived from basic psychodynamic assumptions buttressed by some of her dream material. Her repudiation of my interpretations was, however, coupled with a profound respect for me that was very sustaining for her. An interpretation that she understood and that made her feel good consisted of my pointing out her exceedingly high development of empathic understanding of other people, coupled with an incongruous inability to use this quality in her approach to her own life. This was essentially an interpretation of massive inhibition, and it always made sense to her.

Eventually, patience paid off. She began talking of the blighting effect her depressed mother had produced on her own development, and it was no longer necessary for me to introduce the subject continually. More dramatic was the recall, at this time of increasing insight, of an event that occurred about one year prior to the beginning of her work with me. The patient had arranged to be buried, eventually, next to her dead daughter. But since it was a crowded cemetery, the arrangement was made for the patient to be placed beneath her daughter rather than beside her. That same evening, she dreamed her dead daughter was an infant in a crib; when the patient lifted her out; she discovered herself as an infant underneath her daughter in the crib.

She recalled this grim event and the accompanying dream just as she was achieving greater awareness in the therapy of her fateful early relationship to her mother. This meant that the earlier planting of relatively intellectualized interpretation was now bearing experiential fruit: the awareness of submergence of her own crucial needs to those of others (first mother, then husband, then daughter) recognition of the powerful depressive impact of her mother, the symbolic portrayal of awareness of a layering of her personality structure, and the realization of the necessity of finding her true self under the layers of neurotic traits.

I have presented this as an intellectualized interpretation because when it was initially offered, the patient's conscious response did not include an element of recognition of the essential contents. Yet it had powerful ordering significance for her, which reduced her psychic pain.

Her recall of the cemetery incident and the immediately subsequent dream strongly suggests that the sources of my complex intellectualized interpretation occupied some obscure psychological zone of profound union between her and me, a union of which she and I had been intermittently conscious in the course of our therapeutic relationship. For instance, as the patient was disclosing an incestuous temptation, she asserted that she could only reveal it to me because she knew I would be capable of the same reactions and the same painful struggle with temptation.

I have certain strong but incomplete impressions about the basic passionate impingement between us. My inference is that the tragic loss of her daughter and husband virtually destroyed her fundamental hopeful paradigm of happiness within a family. This message was powerfully conveyed to me, and I reacted powerfully. Sessions in which we sat and cried together as she recounted aspects of her daughter's fatal illness provide a measure of my involvement in her disaster.

My own private fantasy life, especially during early childhood, included much preoccupation with death, disaster, and dishonor. I believe that her terrible anxiety, which had become anarchic despair, was quite infectious. While I sensed her urgent need for hopeful reordering, which I provided in my intellectualized interpretation, I was very probably experiencing a reactivation of my own apocalyptic fantasy activity and was unconsciously soothing myself as I provided the reassuring interpretation to her.

I described her first layer as cheery, but this really represents a very thin and transparent film, barely covering the anguish underlying the surface appearance. In my interpretation, her true self lies beneath the overlying layers of conflict and anguish. Her dream, with its layering, was striking in that as a baby, she lay beneath the daughter. I believe that her dream, which occurred a year before beginning therapy with me, constitutes a powerful confirmation of my interpretation of layering, in two ways. First, because it antedated the interpretation, and second because it was recalled associatively, in response to the interpretation. Both the dream and my interpretation acknowledged that she possessed the will to live, but that it was deeply buried and needed to be excavated. She and I were alike, yet different. We were both fearful and both hopeful. Her fears vastly exceeded her hopes, and my hopes, at least in the therapeutic situation, were considerably greater than my fears.

A sequence of events in this clinical example might be postulated as follows: Initially, the patient brought an overwhelming dread, and I provided a buoyant hopefulness. These polarities unconsciously met, engendering a shared experience of terrible flux that constituted the crucible of mutual transformation. One might assume that during our contacts, we created a shared fantasy characterized by unstable emotions and images, creating a condition of promising ambiguity. After the sessions, as the exciting turbulence subsided, she would find some increase of nondefensive hopefulness, while my outlook became more depressed. Then her depression would resume dominance, and my hopes would again become ascendant. Then we would meet again, once more engaging our antithetical fantasies and needs. Each time the same interaction occurred, and her basic condition gradually changed. So her drama unfolded in a fundamentally happier mode, and I suppose one must assume that mine became more depressed.

While I emphasize the polarized fantasy themes, I should qualify the statement to include the aspect of asymmetry. Her despair was much greater than my joy. The quantity of change in her was also correspondingly much greater than my own.

The death of one's child, at least in contemporary advanced communities, is the most devastating life experience. Such a domestic tragedy colored the patient's life from birth. Her own mother lost her infant son, became chronically depressed, and never recovered. Knudson and I (1960), in our work with the parents of fatally ill children, confirmed the possibility of amelioration, as well as the impossibility of cure. I believe the patient's special vulnerability began with her birth. To some extent she was supposed to replace the dead boy, and initially she did enjoy this role, especially the happiness she provided for her father. But this adaptive defense failed her as she grew and the complex demands of life increased. The precise features of her relationship to her mother remain enigmatic to me—and, I think, to the patient. We do know, however, that as her defensive identification with her father declined, she became more able to feel loving and empathic toward her mother.

I have tried to gather fragments of evidence and to reconstruct our respective minidramas, as well as the joint drama created by their union. This kind of process constitutes the probable intersubjective subtext of effective interpretation.

If assessment of an interpretation is limited to its manifest characteristics, the core meanings may easily be overlooked. Here, for instance, the relation of the interpretation to the union of patient and therapist in the experience of tragic loss, survival anxiety, and despair might have been missed, and the most likely sources of mutative power ignored.

EMPATHIC INTERPRETATIONS

Since all interpretations, to be effective, must ultimately be empathic, this term may seem redundant. It is useful, however, to employ this designation for the class of interpretations that might more correctly be described as primarily affirming or validating the patient's worthiness and lovability. These interpretations at best constitute a spontaneous expression of loving regard for the patient. Empathy includes the therapist's loving understanding of the patient's anger, hatred, and deceitfulness along with the patient's tender and caring attitudes.

Kohut (1977) has provided an extensive study of empathy. His insistence on the need of an empathic-introspective stance by the analyst is his basic technical recommendation. With this approach, the analyst can achieve a more vicarious introspection with regard to the patient. Consequently, the interpretations become very experience-near.

Kohut's appreciation of the overriding importance of an empathic stance and his efforts to establish an appropriate theoretical base for more effective interpretation have stimulated reexamination of the entire issue of interpretation in the therapeutic process. He observes that many patients feel attacked or criticized by standard interpretations of impulse and defense, which in turn often retard rather than facilitate progress. He concludes that this unfortunate circumstance could be avoided by altering both the aim and the form of interpretation. Instead of addressing unconscious drives and defenses against the drives, the analyst should, he believes, maintain a continuously experience-near attitude, from which arise interpretations always closely linked to the patient's subjective state. This focus upon the self provides the base for a drastic revision of the concepts of psychogenesis and the significance of transference. This theory devalues the importance of instinctual drives and fosters a climate of thought conducive to an intersubjective emphasis in interpretation and an associated intersubjective theory of therapeutic action.

Theoretically, Kohut's self-centered approach is compatible with a wide variety of assumptions about the development of self, as well as the interpretive approaches to the self. However, Kohut chose to develop an exceptionally parsimonious and internally consistent theory of the development of the self. This choice reduces, rather than enlarges, the heuristic potential of his work. In terms of interpretation, Kohut dealt with patients' desperate longing for loving admiration, yearning for union with idealized persons, and need for a sense of sharing with a psychological twin. In this perspective, "empathic" interpretations are intended to search out, define, and validate self needs, and generally they subordinate the issues of aggression and sexuality. Although Kohut may not be the original discoverer of such self-centered interpretations, his efforts have been extremely important in revitalizing thought about the self, with beneficial results.

Ironically, Kohut's psychology displays two contradictory tendencies: to be open and yet to foreclose. The primacy of self generates new ways of regarding the suffering patient, thus opening up previously untraveled avenues of thought. It can, however, also promote premature closure by excessive reification of the idea of self. It is a fact, however unwelcome to some, that the ambiguities of psychotherapy vastly exceed the clarities. The therapist best avoids the hazard of premature closure by maintaining a consistently open stance. Overemphasis on the patient's "good" feelings may cause an underestimation of that patient's "meaner" characteristics. This constitutes excessive preoccupation with self needs at the expense of true empathy. Thinking of self, self needs, and self objects engenders new kinds of consciousness in patient and therapist. But focusing only on self issues can create a limited view of therapeutic action.

The Kohutian approach emphasizes the therapist's subjective involvement. Thus far this emphasis has been limited to the therapist's countertransference reactions, instead of including all the therapist's subjective experience. Kohut seems to say that if a transference–countertransference crisis or impasse has occurred, then the therapist's urgent responsibility is to explore his or her own subjective experience. However, once this problem has been resolved, and the necessary transmuting internalization has been resumed, the therapist apparently may assume a more conventional stance, with a markedly reduced interest in the ongoing intersubjective process. This may result in a relative neglect of the therapist's continuing fantasy activity (except during the aforementioned crises). One may therefore be left with an incomplete notion of intersubjectivity and therapeutic action. This reestablishes, however inadvertently, the traditional concept of the therapeutic process as intrapsychic rather than interpersonal and intersubjective.

Empathy requires one indispensable element: the therapist's *ability* to put him- or herself in the patient's position. Without this crucial element, a therapeutic experience will not be significantly based on empathic understanding. This empathic condition constitutes an intersubjective process based upon an underlying identification with the patient. But more is required, since identification may be only unconscious, and the empathic response always includes a conscious component. Identification establishes the possibility, but not the certainty, of feeling with the patient.

The therapist must attend to his or her part of the intersubjective process, and empathy usually follows. This is related to Kohut's concept of "vicarious introspection." The practice of psychotherapy stimulates a fluent mastery of the ability to practice such introspection. The disciplined capacity to put oneself in the patient's place becomes a fundamental component of the therapist's responsive repertoire. An intersubjective approach, however, includes a wider range of involvement than that covered by the term "vicarious introspection."

A powerful countercurrent can occur when the therapist has a disturbing identification with a patient. For example, a heterosexual therapist may achieve empathy with a homosexual patient of the same sex in regard to most issues in the patient's life but become anxious when trying to think and talk about the patient's sexual practices. Feelings of disgust, disapproval, or dislike for the patient should always inform the therapist that a disturbing identification is occurring or being avoided. While identification is essential for empathy, it does not invariably generate empathy. It is obvious in such a circumstance that the therapist's own homosexual wishes are disavowed—hence the identification without empathy. If the therapist can make contact with his own homosexual desires, then empathic availability to the patient may be restored.

The value of so-called empathic interpretations should not be thought to consist of a soothing amorphous resonance which the gifted therapist can achieve after a suitable period of immersion in the mellowing liquidity of Kohut's concepts. Kohut's valuable work points to, but does not elucidate, a highly intimate and powerfully complex psychological substructure that constitutes the hidden fundament of such interpretations. The thorough investigation of this invisible emotional and ideational component extends far beyond the limits of Kohutian theorizing.

The following case examples demonstrate the intersubjective basis of empathic interpretations, that is, interpretations constructed with the deliberate intention of facilitating impeded development.

T. C. is a young, unmarried writer. Her parents never married. While she lived with her mother, she suffered repeated disruptions of relationships with father figures. A sensitive and compassionate woman, she is repeatedly hurt by the men with whom she falls in love. She had been very traumatized by the abandonment by a lover of many years who had promised marriage and then reneged.

She spoke of needing to soothe herself at night with an electric heating pad (her version of a security blanket), and she enjoyed stroking a fuzzy bear doll. I regarded both of these as transitional events. She would experience baffling oscillation of sexual arousal and aversion toward her current lover. When annoyed with him she would sleep upside down in her bed, with her head at the foot of the bed. I regarded this also as a transitional phenomenon.

Much of the symbiotic conflict of this patient was regressive in nature. She had developed an intense oedipal drama with much conflict. The intensity of the regression to mother–daughter pregenital issues was partly due to the striking pathological feature of the various father figures who had passed through her life, and also to the fact that her mother was the only parent consistently present in T. C.'s life from birth to the present.

I concentrated interpretively on the following transitional phenomena. She reported that my comments had become an important source of comfort, which she talked of clutching between sessions. Consequently, I conveyed to her the concept that she was experiencing my words as transitional objects for relief from anxiety over seeking and not finding a reliable father. My actual statement was that she clutched my comments as though they were like her childhood security blanket and that she carried my words like a talisman until she could see me again. Her connection to me as a trustworthy father provided hope for liberation from her traditional suffering within the family. With growing insight, the more or less overt transitional phenomena subsided, and she became more direct in expressing her full range of affects. In addition, her desperate, obsessive fantasies over the lost lover diminished.

In later discussions of the early period of the analysis, T. C. insisted that the richness of her analysis is a direct result of my affirming attitudes and interpretations. She heard the following unstated messages from me during that time: "You are a worthwhile, lovable person. You make many mistakes, but so does everyone, and I will not erroneously focus on them. I appreciate that you are a very complex creature, and although I want to understand you, I possess only limited capabilities; therefore, I am resorting to the next best thing by doing all that I can to keep the analytic situation open and ambiguous. In that way, you and I may be able to achieve fragmentary glimpses of your psychological truths. And we can thereby expect that gradually we will collaboratively assemble the fragments into more complex patterns of self-understanding, but with the certainty that we will never complete the project." This cognitive subtext is obviously saturated with feelings, judgments, and expectations in the analyst that possessed comforting, challenging, and heuristic meanings for the analysand.

T. C. much later informed me that during the first two years of her analysis she began to formulate her analysis in a graphic way, in addition to the intellectual–verbal mode. In fact, this pictorial notion seems gradually to have become a major, but not exclusive or dominant, mode of experiencing the analysis. She described abstract forms, with subdued and shadowy colors. Both forms and colors were fluid. The forms might tend toward a sphere and then flow into some other shifting, three-dimensional shape. Similarly, the colors would merge, blend, transform. T. C. is convinced that her visual, graphic experience of the analysis is more than just her idiosyncratic, artistic mode of ego integration. She believes that the structure of my interpretations contained at least some of the components of her visual patterns, although I was unaware of this. Consistently, throughout the analysis, she has noted my colorful, image-laden language, as well as my references to works of art, poetry, drama, and history. It seems probable that in various ways, I was exerting pressure upon her to utilize and enjoy her own creative inclinations and resources. She is confident that these influences by me were interpretations, without words, that enabled her to feel more like a part of the world rather than like an alienated, illegitimate little girl. An interpretation, then, may be viewed as like a dream—the explicit elements are only a small part of the total. Interpretations, like dreams, require interpretations.

The most consistent intersubjective phenomenon in the analysis of T. C. has been and continues to be maximal reciprocal trust. Neither of us can conceive of betrayal by the other. As she puts it, "You have never made an interpretation that seemed attacking." We share a naive wide-eyed innocence, constantly incorporating the world, and attempting to alleviate all pain in the world. This infantile grandiosity is ultimately derived from a powerful identification with an adored, but feared, mother. I have repeatedly observed a remarkable paradox in my attitude to her. I focus on her need to achieve a more valid and stable sense of self, but I do so by trying to bring the universe of events and meanings to our dialogue. This succeeds, but not in a neat and readily explainable way. Our experience is drenched with empathy. In the phase of the analysis described here, the empathy drew heavily from a massive reciprocal maternal identification.

TRANSFERENCE INTERPRETATIONS

Transference influences all interpretations to some extent. Transference interpretations focus primarily on the meanings of the therapeutic relationship. They deal with data generated in the therapy and directly experienced by both participants. These data constitute a rich resource for understanding the patient's psychological life.

Premature transference interpretations invariably breed resistance in the patient because they actually contain disruptive subtextual messages much different from their overt content. Poorly timed transference interpretations arise from specific and potentially identifiable processes occurring in the therapist. One such dissonant motive would be the analyst's anxiety over not being manifestly at the center of the patient's attention.

In order to establish suitable conditions for the evocation and amplification of therapeutic transference, certain responsibilities devolve upon the therapist. The therapist must avoid the therapeutic misfortune of objectifying the patient and his special characteristics. This goal is best achieved through the intersubjective imperative, which requires that the therapist consistently recognize in him- or herself fears and yearnings analogous to those perceived in the patient.

This sense of mutuality is implicitly conveyed to the patient, who experiences an intense response. Often this response is consciously positive, but often it is not. Some patients may consciously distrust, even repudiate, this important implied message. But so long as the patient is able to sustain this negation within the safe frame of therapy, without abrogating the frame, the negative response itself constitutes a powerful transforming force.

The sense of mutuality is the appropriate circumstance for the optimal evocation and amplification of therapeutic transference. The therapist thereby invites the patient to experience a new kind of intimacy, one that is creative and beyond conventional restraints. The therapist maintains an uninterrupted appreciation of his or her own analogous needs; thus the therapist can vicariously appreciate the patient's obligatory struggle against the new. The therapist's inevitable limitations, however, result in an instability of response, involving varying degrees of anxiety, guilt, and irritation. The self-analysis of these reactions and *judicious* discussion of them with the patient promotes maintenance in the therapist of a satisfactory state of identification and empathy.

This is the intense, intersubjective field from which mutative transference interpretations arise. The fundamental fantasies of both parties interact, producing the conditions for timely transference interpretation. And it is not just a matter of the intermittent activation of the therapist's countertransference; the therapist's fantasy life is consistently and coequally involved in this process.

A 29-year-old single female junior business executive offered a family portrait that portrayed her mother as the destructive center of the family. As a result of the patient's negativistic attitudes during mid-adolescence, the mother forced the patient to leave home and attend boarding school. The patient felt that her father loved her but in critical moments submitted to his wife's dictates under the guise of being a loyal husband. The patient had a younger brother who had been spared the worst ravages of the maternal aggression.

After a year of therapy, the patient reported a dream that she described as constituting a "true epiphany" for her. It went as follows:

> My mother has died—drowned in the ocean. My father is walking on the beach with a young blond woman in a black bathing suit.

The patient felt that she wished her mother's death for venal reasons and that she was the blond who replaced the mother with her father. Previously she had regarded herself only as the victim of her neurotic mother's aggression. She now recognized, through the dream, her oedipally based wish to kill her mother and replace her mother as her father's mate.

During a recent holiday visit to her parent's home, she had been pleasantly surprised to find her mother unusually warm and affirming of the patient's adult, feminine interests. As the dream converged with the new discovery, the patient became more aware of the destructive role of her oedipal wishes. The session was lively and, I thought, productive. Yet the patient entered my office the next time telling me that she had been hurt and dismayed by my lack of enthusiasm for her "epiphany."

When I had earlier inquired about her thoughts about me, she always insisted that she needed to perceive me only as avuncular, competent, and wise. She felt that if she acknowledged my more ignoble traits, she would be unable to reveal to me her petty, inconsistent, ambivalent qualities. Although numerous signs of transference had surfaced during this early period, I regularly made the judgment that interpreting them would be premature and probably disruptive. Now, however, she was accusing me of hurting her in precisely the mode that her mother had so often hurt her. Furthermore, she voiced this feeling at the very same time she was feeling better toward her mother and able to appreciate how she had wished to hurt her mother.

When I pointed out that these feelings toward me were obviously derived from her feelings about her mother, she readily concurred. I added that this was the first occasion when we had been able mutually to recognize feelings about me that derived from her family problems. Again she happily agreed, adding that she could now experience me as a real person with variegated traits. I made the further general point that the reappropriation of disowned aggression can often be very liberating.

She returned to her next session with a dream that I was having an affair and that she was helping me but was not my lover. She chose to focus on the dream as further expression of her newfound capacity to acknowledge my humanness, and she specifically disclaimed any erotic feelings toward me. Despite the obvious erotic implication for the transference, I once again prudently decided not to challenge her view.

While the therapist should continuously monitor the state of the transference during psychotherapy, there are certain conditions that indicate the pressing need for transference interpretation. These include painful affect of obscure origin when it is blocking therapeutic progress, intensification of the patient's manifest interest in the therapeutic process or the therapist, and direct or thinly veiled reference to the therapist in dreams and fantasies. Stylistic considerations are important. For example, some patients, for lengthy periods, have great difficulty discussing the patient-therapist relationship directly; others do so enthusiastically from the outset of therapy. Skillful therapists adapt their interpretive approach to the patient.

Early in therapy, the patient had a defensive pattern of charming flightiness. With progress in treatment the defense diminished, and she recognized that her previous pattern had been an aspect of a false self that she had employed to avoid knowing her true feelings and thoughts. It was then that she became able to acknowledge her responsibilities in the conflicts with her mother. As a corollary, she developed disappointment and anger toward me. The interpretation of hostility in the transference was necessary to preserve and facilitate the therapy.

The patient became able openly to express negative feelings toward me, and I, in my interpretation, suggested the link to her mother. She then confirmed that they were the same kinds of feelings she had toward her mother. In my interpretation I had conveyed certain important messages to her that were subtextual. When I pointed out that we were now able to experience our first mutual recognition of her transference feelings about me, I was also conveying other ideas to her: that she had hitherto feared telling me the psychological truth, that I really wanted to hear her truth, that I would absorb these emotional realities, and that I would eventually respond to her in ways that were enriched, rather than depleted, by her disclosure of hostility toward me.

By expressing her hostility, she was requesting that I subtextually tell her that I wanted truth, not appeasement. This would be the equivalent of my telling her that I valued her autonomy rather than her symbiotic submission. So in my unqualified acceptance of her, I was also expressing another idea of great importance: I will not let you down as your father did, but I will help you use your hostile feelings to enlarge your self-understanding.

The patient steadily reduced her defensively positive attitude to me, as my responses encouraged her trust. She was able to relax and share with me the more complete range of hopes, fears, resentments, beliefs, and other attitudes. Many unstated potential ideas in the therapeutic transaction are first expressed by a patient as feeling states. In productive intersubjective conjunction, these may be returned by the therapist in more explicit verbal form as ideas or interpretations. For example, she had previously needed to have only general trusting and positive feelings for me because she feared that if she revealed her more complex and ambivalent attitudes, I would no longer accept her.

My internal experience of her early defensive "positive" attitude toward me had, I think, been the fairly typical reactions of a reasonably sensitive, perceptive therapist. The net effect upon me was one of feeling rather desperately needed, but this feeling was always laced with a feeling of uncertainty and anxiety about the genuineness of the patient's attitudes. Recurrent silent questions would occur to me: "Is she telling me what really happened, how she really felt? Why does she so assiduously avoid any of the specifics of her sexual life?" I noticed some old, unwelcome feelings associated with being the poor, depreciated Jewish boy who is momentarily accepted but is in continuous jeopardy of being swept back into the dustbin of rejection. These feelings suggested to me that I was experiencing a similar pain in her, and I was able to refine my interpretive responses to her. Indirectly, it became apparent to me that her basic, rather than defensive, faith in my trustworthiness was now greatly increased as she was dealing with her hostility. I experienced a deeper level of painful ideas and helped her face her own self-negation. I consciously felt her pain in my own idiom, and I could perceive its relevance to her suffering.

When I faced and accepted my narcissistic vulnerability with this patient, I was able to perceive more clearly and completely the network of ideas that clustered under the surface of the troubled relationship of mother and daughter. Ironically, her mother, who might have helped the patient by using her own pain with her own mother, had instead followed the path of repression and projection. This had led inevitably to the terrible chronic impasse between her and the patient.

In my interpretation I clearly, although subtextually, told her that she and her mother had become enemies early in the patient's life because of her mother's dishonesty with herself. This fundamental fact had caused the mother, as she tried to deny her rage and disappointment with her own mother, to feel the same awful mother–daughter tensions in her relationship with my patient. The patient then told me of a dream in which her mother served a horrible egg soufflé, made in dishwater. This dream reflected a deep frustration with the mother's inability to provide a nurturing empathy. Thus another implicit idea in my interpretation was that the patient hated and distrusted her mother for inadequate mothering and the attempt to use the patient as a narcissistic extension of her own troubled and defective self.

My subjective experience was essential to my therapeutic understanding of this patient. The interpretations derived from my intimate involvement as well as from my work identity and my professional experience. The transference being created by both persons in the analytic situation is a powerful force in the evocation of the analyst's subjectivity, rendering it potentially available to consciousness, and illuminating its intersubjective relevance. Transference is a very important manifestation of the intersubjective process. And transference always contributes to the development of interpretation, whether or not it is the explicit focus of the particular interpretation.

INTERPRETATIONS LINKING THERAPEUTIC REALITY AND TRANSFERENCE: INTERPRETATION AND THERAPIST ERROR

The interpretive use of therapists' idiosyncrasies can be very interesting and useful. The following case illustrates this type of interpretation.

A young female patient entered therapy because of anxiety, loneliness, and self-doubt. She had been abandoned by her father when she was an infant, and her mother had frequently been ill. From earliest childhood, ethical issues played a conspicuous part in her relationships. She was deeply appreciative of her mother's struggle to provide a humanistic environment for her children. The numerous childhood memories regularly converged to portray a child who was exceptionally responsible from a very early age, but who, nevertheless, was trapped by the experiential limitations of her tender age. This circumstance enhanced helpless, vulnerable, and guilty feelings, which intensified an inner pressure to do well. She became academically and socially successful. Self-interest, however, was always subordinated to the interests of others. She decided to become a writer in order to "give" to humanity, and following college she did in fact enjoy a successful writing career.

While still in her early twenties, she elected to change course and study for a doctorate in an academic specialty, in which endeavor she is achieving increasing recognition.

When I first met her, I perceived her as warm, enthusiastic, and open. I judged her to be quite ingenuous, with a naive and partly defensive belief in the powers of psychoanalysis. I assumed that she would eventually become disillusioned, and I wondered silently whether this disillusionment would destroy her analysis, or whether it would contribute to her analytic wisdom.

Even at that early time, I knew that a profound cynicism growing in me about the human condition influenced my judgment. In part, my impression of her naïveté was distorted by my own preoccupations, which nevertheless sensitized me to a powerful existential issue for the patient. Although I correctly perceived the childlike, naive aspect of her faith in analysis and her conviction of the possibility of human happiness, at the same time I defensively underestimated her realism and sophistication. My inner struggle alerted me to hers, and it also created some false perceptions in me.

Her conspicuous emphasis on fairness, kindness, and generosity resonated powerfully with similar values in me. Some important meanings of these qualities were a desire to emulate her mother, a wish to relieve mother's suffering as mother had done for her, a loving concern for siblings—as well as reaction formations against her hostile attitudes toward them. Her subjective sense of self was fluid, since it depended on her degree of success in these efforts.

On a cold, blustery day, this patient came for her regular appointment. She was tired and irritable from overwork, financial worries, and indecision about whether to marry. As she lay on the couch, she sadly recalled how in her love relationships, she always became involved, while the man avoided complete commitment, and she felt kept at a distance. That day the office was exceptionally chilly. As my hands were dry and itchy, I applied some hand cream and began to rub my hands together while we were talking. The patient heard the activity, began to feel very rejected, and said, "You want to wash your hands of me."

I interpreted to her that her lifelong fears of loss and abandonment generated her chronic anxiety, propelled her into relationships with men who would keep her at arm's length (repetition compulsion), and even caused her to have transference distortions of the same nature to the therapist.

Therapists should not deliberately provoke patients, but for various reasons provocations may occur. The likely patient response is to feel hurt, angry, misunderstood, rejected. The therapist's options are to interpret the patient's response, acknowledge the reality basis for the patient's reaction, or both. The choice depends upon the strength and suppleness of the therapeutic relationship and upon the current defensive state of the patient.

In this instance, I chose to interpret the patient's reactions; no reality acknowledgment was necessary. In regard to my hand rubbing and its unconscious implications, my omission of any reference to wrongdoing on my part conveyed some very specific ideas to the patient. Among these ideas was my opinion that she had a deep trust in me. On this basis, therefore, I assumed she knew that I would spontaneously seek and discover the unconscious meaning of my acting out and she could therefore openly reveal her hurt feelings of being rejected by me without fear of a defensively punitive response from me. An acknowledgment of culpability by me would have been redundant and therefore defensive (since redundancy is a defense against anxiety). The patient's basic trust promotes truthful resonance in the therapeutic relationship and induces an inner state of relaxation in the therapist in which the therapist feels a kind of unconditional acceptance by the patient. Self-indictments or self-exculpations by the therapist, under these conditions, are inappropriate and disruptive and would convey to the patient the message, "I fear you."

Out of my free and safe feelings with this patient, I became able to develop a more conscious formulation of traits I had intuitively appreciated from the outset of the analysis. A body of essentially subtextual ideas developed and changed as our relationship evolved, and I believe I conveyed them to the patient implicitly or subtextually, rather than in my manifest communications.

Was the application of skin cream an error? The more important question is, what did the act mean, and did it become a useful analytic event? My retrospective analysis leads me to conclude that I was acting out an unconscious identification with the patient's mother, whose health had preoccupied the patient for many years. And I was probably expressing the thought that the patient should take care of me. Her response, "You want to wash your hands of me," is particularly interesting if it is regarded as an accusation that I, like Pontius Pilate, was avoiding my moral responsibility to her. Yet I doubted the depth of her accusation. Instead, I believe the subtext of her accusation was a response to the implicit aspect of my hand rubbing. When I behaved like the sick mother, I was restating the moral power and problems in the mother–daughter relationship. She, on the other hand, in her irritable accusation, was actually expressing her love and gratitude to a mother who sustained the family throughout various disruptions, notwithstanding her suffering from physical illnesses.

These feelings were juxtaposed with the patient's individual needs for undistracted and unencumbered love and care, creating a dilemma over how much to expect or demand from a significant other. Since her mother provided hope and security, the patient did not wish or dare to damage that vital resource. Out of all this, she learned to become a good, empathic family member in order to maintain an equilibrium. As she grew, this childhood moral dilemma and its adaptive consequences became a prominent character trait in her adult life. So when the patient responded to me with a charge of moral irresponsibility, she was assuring me that she heard the submerged moral communication in my hand rubbing, and was returning to the subject of her problems with men.

My verbal interpretations addressed her fears of abandonment by men, beginning with her father in infancy, continuing with men who had been lovers, and now occurring with me. The fact of the loss of her father, virtually from birth, may fairly be regarded as the prototypic basis for her exceptional awareness of psychological suffering. Her reaction to the loss of her father became the enabling event for her tremendous empathic capabilities, with some disturbing complications. No matter how caring and compassionate she might be, her unconscious dynamics have always required that she sustain a sense of empathic moral insufficiency with consequent guilt feeling, which in turn engender expectations of rejections by men. The problem of the lost father underlay and permeated the moral problems in the mother–daughter relationship, even though the maternal issues were more blatant in this transference event.

The incident of the hand rubbing constituted a memorable event in the analysis. In this behavior, I made a powerful set of statements. Although my action was not consciously intended to be therapeutic, it nevertheless can be regarded as an interpretation, albeit a nonverbal one. This would illustrate why it is desirable to extend the concept of interpretation beyond strictly verbal limits.

In effect, I gradually "told" her the above ideas. I place "told" in quotes, because these thoughts were unstated communications. Eventually, I did discuss all this in considerable detail. When I did so, she confirmed my strong impression that she already knew these ideas of mine.

Moral issues are of great importance in all analyses. They achieve particular clarity in cases such as this one, in which a moral-philosophical tone continuously pervades the analytic transactions. Such moral emphasis—both explicit and implicit—can have identifiably different effects upon the analyst. If the moral pressure generates undue anxiety in the therapist, he or she will probably attempt to deal with the defensive meaning for the patient prematurely in the effort to cope with his or her own anxiety. Here the implicit message (idea) conveyed by the therapist would be as follows: "You are bothersome to bring up these moral dilemmas continually. It is impractical, childlike, and objectionable to continue doing this. Only immature children keep wondering about ultimate meanings. I will be more comfortable and I will be more approving of you if you stop this and become more pragmatic."

Alternatively, if the therapist accepts the apparently infinite regress of each moral dilemma leading to a new one, which then produces another, and so on, a different message (idea) is conveyed from analyst to patient: "No final answers are available to us; it is the process of life that is important; as we strive to deal with each present problem a new one is being generated, and this is how we create new human meanings in this ambiguous, emerging world of relationships."

In the fifth year of the analysis, the patient began to describe her experience of the analysis as abstract forms that were continuously shifting. She said that I had contributed to this perception by the implicit message in my interpretations. I requested that she record her impressions of this nonverbal experience, and she provided the following "Picture of the Analytic Process":

The "canvas" is fluid and three-dimensional. Different forms appear and disappear. They are of varying hues and shapes. The forms appear as representations of verbal, emotional, or intellectual concepts. At times they coalesce, creating new forms, or they may touch and separate as they were or into new and different forms. They have a softness in their substance. These appearing forms—some newly created, some newly defined or re-created—are of the same matrix as is the composition of the fluid canvas. Yet at times they may seem to be of different substance such as playful soap bubbles in air, or shapes of oil droplets on water's surface. There is a sense of discovery.

The picture is reminiscent of a dream where I was floating on water face down. Contact with people on shore was constant, even when my attention shifted to the presence and discovery of the deep. The body of water was a combination swimming pool and ocean.

In the past, it felt as if my experience was confined to being aware of only a few forms. These forms seemed to be the "canvas," not just part of a larger whole. In this way, the current experience feels more expansive.

These shifting visual images represent the various moral concerns just described. Thus, it does seem that the patient's painful immersions in an endless series of moral dilemmas eventuates in a transformed, enriched, and expanded human experience through the mediating effect of the analyst's active attunement to the moral questioning. This mediation involves the counterpart activation of old and new moral problems of the analyst. The analyst attempts to make appropriate therapeutic responses, but each such response is saturated with the analyst's own passionate preoccupations. This process can occur even when the analyst is quite austere in his or her verbal activity.

This account illustrates the enormous psychological richness that inheres in a bit of superficially ordinary acting out by the analyst. The transferential correlates of these therapeutic realities can be elucidated with great therapeutic benefit. Although this example was selected from a long and intensive psychoanalytic situation, the same principles operate in all exploratory treatment situations.

INTERPRETATION OF RESISTANCE

Resistance is the condition in which passionately held ideas do not pass freely between patient and therapist. The therapist's subjective experience is an indispensable ingredient in recognizing resistance; when the therapist feels frustration, boredom, distractibility, fatigue, and self-doubt, the therapeutic communication is seriously obstructed.

Interpreting resistance is a complex and important issue that obtains in all therapy aimed at self-transformation through insight and enhanced consciousness. Interpretation of resistance does *not* mean telling a patient that he or she is resisting. In fact, therapists should scrupulously avoid using the term "resistance" in their remarks to patients. As Schafer (1983) has noted, "resisting is not opposing the analysis . . . but rather [is] the analysand's next significant step in the analytic process" (p. 171). The following account illustrates one way in which therapists can utilize the interpretation of resistance.

> A middle-aged, overweight man came to therapy primarily because of depression, but he also complained of various phobias such as fear of flying and strange hotel rooms. He dreamed repetitively of vomiting and of searching futilely through corridors and rooms of large hotels. He was very unhappy in his third marriage, and although he was extremely successful, he felt burdened by his multitudinous responsibilities and anticipated a dreadful collapse of his business.
>
> The patient felt increasingly alienated from work, family, and friends, but he believed no one was aware of this. He was able to maintain a façade of warmth, humor, and

charm and was, he believed, considered everyone's "best friend"—yet he felt utterly friendless and alone. The patient thought he did not lose weight because whenever he began mentally to picture himself as a slim, virile man, he became anxious, even panicky. But he did not understand this reaction.

His mother had been a chronically drug-dependent invalid from the time of his late childhood, and the patient early on assumed a caretaking, self-sacrificing role within the family. His colorful, narcissistic, and manipulative father enjoyed his life without apparent concern about the semi-invalid, regressed mother.

Early in therapy the patient focused on his father and throughout therapy he maintained a low-key amused, exasperated affection for the irascible, irrepressible, and irresponsible father. At no time was the equivalent quality of humor evident toward the mother, whose disorder gradually replaced the father's as the dominant historical theme of the analytic therapy.

Although I perceived the patient's pathological unconscious maternal identification in all this, I was initially unable to mobilize mutative forces. As the months wore on, I began to notice a profound discontinuity. He often felt relief during a session from some interpretation of mine, but I never knew from one session to the next what his condition would be. This circumstance coexisted with a striking lack of spontaneous thematic continuity in his associations. That is, even a powerful interpretation in the previous session would not be alluded to in the following one.

I constructed a meaning from this and said to the patient: "Basically you are struggling against recognition of an unconscious identification with your sick mother. You not only loved her, but you hated her, and you felt very guilty toward her. Yet she and your crucial memories of her are a vital part of you, despite your struggle against this realization. So long as you are unable to recognize that she exists as part of you, you will be correspondingly crippled in your life. The recognition and acceptance of her in you will be very strengthening." He experienced this as a very important insight and said that even though we had previously discussed an identification with her and how her chronic invalidism had damaged his life, he had only now become able to appreciate consciously that an active part of him consisted of her.

When he came for his next session, he announced that his depression had greatly subsided, but as usual, he made no effort to connect this session with the previous one, even though I felt that the events that had transpired in the hour before were the basis for his improvement. I extended the preceding interpretation with this follow-up: I suggested that his inability to connect contiguous sessions in our dialogue arose from his prior inability to experience consciously his deep identification with his mother. In fact, I averred, by maintaining a discontinuity of the sessions, he had been able to retard progress toward awareness of the maternal identification. I suggested that maintaining the discontinuities of this therapeutic behavior represented his acting out of his identification with his disorganized mother. (Furthermore, I thought, but did not state, that to the extent his neurotic behavior in the therapy reduced my effectiveness, it might also be intended to make me into the ineffectual mother.) But now, I proposed, since he had become aware of this identification and its disabling consequences, he might be more able to maintain consciousness of the therapeutic process. He understood this, considered it accurate and liberating, and began showing considerably more continuity between sessions.

My interpretations of the complex set of attitudes toward the sick mother had a striking effect on the psychotherapy. Not only did the patient become more conscious of the therapeutic process and thus more attentive to continuity of sessions, but a dramatic change also occurred in his consciousness of his mother and of his relationship to her. For example, he began saying that for the first time, he realized emotionally that his mother is dead, although she had been dead for over two decades.

We both speculated that his obesity, which was especially characterized by a very large abdomen, expressed a fantasy of carrying his mother's body within him. He also reported a diminution of his vomiting dreams, which we thought might express an unsuccessful effort to disgorge the mother, while simultaneously showing his deep disgust over her serious failures as the mothering person in his life. He began requiring more appropriate mothering behavior by his infantile wife toward their children, and he was able to reduce somewhat his uncontrollable compulsive mothering behavior toward people who became close figures in his life.

My inner resonance with this man became clarified with time. I have an early childhood memory of standing at a large window in a bleak, sun-drenched room, chewing a crust of Jewish rye bread, awaiting the return of my mother, who may have been away earning money for basic expenses. This was the modest apartment of my mother's friend, who was babysitting me. This mildly unpleasant memory was evoked by the patient. My mother was as endlessly active as his mother was inert. My inner thoughts were of the harsh domestic reality that called forth my mother's purposeful activity, and I could feel empathy for his disgust (the vomiting dreams) over his nonfunctional and unattractive mother. Yet I also reflected silently that my mother's enforced absences (or so it seemed) deprived me of sufficient mothering. The rage over this deprivation was reflected in my childhood anxiety and irritability and in a childhood fantasy that my mother's abdominal fat pannus contained an ossified, long-dead fetus. There is a less clear memory that I had urges to rip out that poor dead interloper. I do not know whether this inclination was intended to overkill my rival for mothering, or whether it was a nobler wish to restore to my mother her original beauty, or an ignoble urge to kill her.

When I spoke to the patient, fundamentally I was silently telling him that I regarded him as a variant of my infuriatingly fat-bellied mother. Not only did he resemble her physically, but his devotion to caretaking, however irritably practiced, also was like hers. Such basic concepts in the therapist are ineluctably communicated to the patient. I was also (non-verbally) telling him that his trust in my interpretations, by revealing his psychological truths, enabled me to understand better the frustrating lapses in my mother's caretaking capabilities. So another submerged message from me to him was that he could construct a more valid self by relinquishing his resistive obsession with his mother. I may also have conveyed to him the notion that, since we were each engaged in a chronic and painful struggle with our mothers, we could support one another and thus reduce, if not eliminate, our problems. Although his prevailing manifest attitudes toward me were closest to those of a street-smart kid brother to a beloved, scholarly, trusted older brother, the mother–son conflict did color our relationship in an additional way.

It is quite possible that this ebullient man stimulated me to think of my mother with the large abdomen, as though in his arrival, she was once more trudging up Market Street in the harsh, chilling sunlight as I, dissembling, met her with an inward smile and a hidden profound dread of another disappointment. Could I possibly have concealed the essence of my search for mothering from this man, with whom I shared such resonance? At one point in the therapy, the patient told me he understood everything. I knew he meant that he knew what I did not say as well as what I did say. I believe this degree of closeness reflects an unconscious fantasy in each of us, holding close the insufficient or absent mother. Furthermore, my interpretations to him included this latent idea that he was holding close the impaired mother, and that the result was an aching feeling of inner emptiness.

AFFECT-LADEN INTERPRETATIONS

Affect-laden interpretations serve the primary purpose of releasing emotion, which, in its blockage, obstructs analytic progress. When suitably framed and delivered, such interpretations stimulate more active experiencing and expressing of affect, with consequent facilitation of the analytic process.

These interpretations like all others, arise ultimately from an intersubjective source.

Sam, a professional writer, was in his late fifties when he came to therapy to try to deal with various problems, including phobic anxiety over flying and open spaces, insufficiently assertive behavior in most relationships, and anguish over undue submissiveness to older men. He had a violent alcoholic father, and as a child had lost his best friend in a terrible "accident."

Jimmy and Sam were 4 years old when Jimmy was killed. Their parents were close friends. Sam's father worked in Jimmy's father's sawmill, and Jimmy's family lived just up the mountain from Sam's. Jimmy and Sam were the closest of friends, even alter egos. At that time, each was an only child. One day, Jimmy's mother took her squirrel gun behind the house, took aim, and mistakenly blew Jimmy's brains out. Sam could never forget the horrible scene of the mother in agony, staggering down the mountainside past his home, the body of her son in her arms, blood over her head, arms, and dress, moaning, "I've killed my baby."

While the little community was shocked over the accident, Sam felt that everyone knew it was not really accidental. Jimmy had been conceived and born prior to the parents' marriage, and Sam always believed that guilt over her sin caused the mother to shoot Jimmy. No one ever openly discussed this version of the tragedy.

Sam additionally had major problems over the event. He identified with Jimmy and was terrified. He felt great relief that Jimmy, and not he, was the victim, and he felt enormous guilt. For years thereafter, when Sam masturbated, he would have the illusion that the ejaculate on his hand was blood—Jimmy's blood on his hand.

After World War II, Sam's closest buddy from the army killed himself by firing a gun into his head. Furthermore, before seeing me, Sam had been in treatment with another male therapist who experienced a major head injury, also accidental but questionable. After this injury, the therapist

was somewhat impaired. Sam's confidence in him plum-
meted, and he began therapy with me.

At the time I was seeing him, Sam was a heavy smoker
with a persistent cough. He feared that he had a serious lung
disease. However, a visit to a pulmonologist revealed no
illness, and the patient asked if I could help him break the
smoking habit.

When Sam paid his very first visit to me, he initiated the
use of hands and figures in our dialogue. At that time, he
deplored his excessively meek and obsequious attitudes toward others he perceived as powerful. He called himself
Uriah Heep and mockingly wrung his hands and fingers in
imitation of that caricature of sinister submissiveness.

The patient and I shared many features. We were the
same age and came from similar mountainous regions, he
from the Ozarks and I from Appalachia. We dealt with people
in similar ways, both having struggled to become more self-
assertive in our relationships. Like the patient, I had been a
confirmed smoker for many years. Unlike him, however, I
had quit smoking ten years before this therapeutic encounter.
I was able to discard cigarettes only when I realized that not
smoking was an expression of freedom and self-fulfillment,
rather than of discipline and self-deprivation—a reversal of
the usual assumption.

In the course of his first year in therapy, Sam had re-
linquished much of his appeasing, submissive behavior. I now
told him that by smoking, he was making himself the victim
of the hot, searing, charring smoke—an evil, destructive va-
por emitted by the same witch or devil parent who had always
terrorized him into submission. I grimaced and moved my
arms and hands in a writhing, menacing way as I made these
remarks. He was startled and bemused—and he promptly
stopped smoking! This cessation was not lasting. Only at a
later time did he succeed in stopping permanently. However,
this episode was important because it marked the beginning
of the process of relinquishing cigarettes.

My mode of intervention could be regarded as acting
out that was unnecessary and potentially damaging. Or it

could be seen as an example of Alexander's (1946) "corrective emotional experience." However, neither of these explanations approximates the real meaning of this transaction for the patient and for me. This joint meaning elucidates a central theme—the powerful interplay of interpretive meaning for both participants in the psychotherapeutic transaction.

My affect-laden interpretation involving the patient's health is part of a network of therapeutic events that extended back to the early phase of therapy. During the very earliest months of the treatment, Sam enjoyed a growing sense of comfort and acceptance, thus reinforcing the initial sense of consanguinity. He then was able to tell me of a recurrent nightmare that had begun at age 4 following Jimmy's death and persisted to the present:

> My mother, Jimmy's mother, and I are in a hollow, near a trestle. It is a glade with rich soil, which I know very well. The women are digging up Boston ferns that grow there. I am running about frantically through the bushes and tall grass, hoping I can find Jimmy, to warn him that his mother is going to kill him. Suddenly, a black snake appears; it is very menacing. Mother, Jimmy's mother, and I flee. I am terrified, and I awaken.

This dream began after Jimmy's violent death, and it represented Sam's effort, hitherto unsuccessful, to master the deep trauma of that event. I heard this story of anguish in early childhood with sympathetic pain. If I had any doubt that I identified with Jimmy, as well as with Sam, it was soon dispelled. For, as Sam recounted these horrors, I would picture, with mixed anxiety and amusement, my brains blown out along my line of baldness, like Jimmy's.

Now, in retrospect, I understand that my dramatized interpretation was even more affect laden than I initially realized. I joined Sam in my concern over lung disease. This may also have represented identification with Jimmy, the cigarettes symbolizing the "smoking gun." I told him, in effect, that I, like he, but unlike Jimmy, was also a survivor.

As I graphically portrayed the smoke snaking its way down his windpipe, I took on the role of evil, the snake of the dream symbolizing aggression and sexuality, driving *all* before it, out of the garden. I felt all this along with Sam, but my full realization has taken several years to catch up with my behavior.

Although the dramatized smoking interpretation occurred approximately two years after the snake dream, the same issues were being worked with in the separate events. Sam was convinced (and I cannot challenge his opinion) that when he did not smoke, he was unable to write. He attributed the inhibition to a certain cerebral fogginess and an inability to focus on ideas. My view is that the smoking was an oral masochistic defense that relieved his dread of being destroyed. When I tell him that he can be free of the lethal mother by joining me in not smoking, he may also unconsciously believe that I am Jimmy and that he can join me only in death.

After the earlier report of the dream and the tragic history of Jimmy, we made considerable progress with respect to this issue. The recurrent nightmare stopped—*after over fifty years*. And we went on to analyze his profound fear of his eruptive alcoholic father. The result was a marked reduction in his free-floating and phobic anxiety, as well as an increased assertiveness.

As in the rest of life development, each powerful therapeutic event colors all subsequent experiences. With time, I achieved increasing comfort with *my* transient therapeutic identification with Jimmy. I was reminded of the mysterious death or disappearance of a pretty little schoolmate when I was 5 or 6. We, her classmates, were told that she died of an infection during the summer vacation between kindergarten and the first grade. This memory constituted my counterpart to Sam's memories of Jimmy.

Thus, in my smoking interpretation to Sam I was saying that we children can overcome the damaging, even lethal, effects of conflicted, incompetent, or hostile parents and their surrogates. While Sam loved his parents, he had serious doubts about their nurturing capabilities. These doubts coexisted with tremendous nostalgic respect for "the family." So an important subtextual message in my animated interpretation was that we boys must rely upon ourselves rather than put uncritical faith in our parents, and thereby I was urging him to relinquish his defensive idealization of his parents. From the time of Jimmy's death, Sam had been shocked and frightened by the adult hypocrisy surrounding the tragedy. Jimmy's parents, Sam's parents, the Baptist minister, the sheriff, and all the others knew Jimmy's death was unconsciously motivated murder, but no one openly acknowledged it, and they all expressed the same view that Jimmy's death was God's will and for the best.

My underlying message to Sam in the smoking interpretation dealt with the betrayal, or sacrifice, of children on the altar of parental and societal conflict. I was urging him to relinquish his role of inflicting sacrificial wounds upon himself through the penitential act of smoking. My capability for this interpretive act arose from my dual symbolic role as Jimmy, who died, as well as the surviving and liberated, nonsmoking alter ego.

Approximately two years after the smoking interpretation, Sam, on one of his periodic visits to his childhood home in the Ozarks, had finally gathered enough courage to visit Jimmy's grave for the first time since childhood. He brought me a photograph of the headstone, which referred to Jimmy as a lamb. I regarded this designation as corroborative of Jimmy's role as sacrificial object.

The second case involved a married woman, Alicia, born and reared in the Middle West. She had felt limited warmth from both her parents. Her mother was a somewhat cold but submissive person with whom she went regularly to fashionable tearooms for lunch. Her father, on the other hand, was aggressive, even domineering. She recalled that his behavior with her was definitely sexualized, including hugs with his erect penis pressed against her. She experienced him as invasive and not really loving. Despite her serious emotional isolation, this woman was an accomplished professional person, ambitious and productive. She was married and had an adolescent daughter. She seemed finicky and behaved as though she feared being messy or being attacked.

At the outset, the patient came twice a week and sat up. She had much difficulty maintaining contact with me. As we moved into discussion of emotionally charged matters, she would typically lose contact with me and the subject. It was clear that she could not cope with intense and open emotion; she simply shut down and became silent. After a number of minutes, or in the following session, we would be able to resume conversation. This striking dissociative phenomenon subsided after several months. By this time we were meeting four times weekly, and the patient began using the couch.

This phase of the treatment moved very slowly, although she behaved in a diligent and conscientious manner. Her grossly dissociative episodes disappeared, and she handled some frightening family crises with skill, including her daughter's severe depression during late adolescence. Her professional skills also grew.

While she was obviously attached to me, I had persistent difficulty understanding the ongoing therapeutic process. I frequently had the silent thought that she was too intelligent for me, that I was not endowed to deal with the high level of her abstract thinking. My usual impression (and frequent interpretation) was that she was emotionally isolated and intellectualized in a defensive way. But I often wondered if perhaps I was thinking and saying this only to preserve my self-esteem in the presence of a superior person. I now realize that these were indications of a faltering sense of self in me that arose from the powerful but inaccessible dynamics of that analytic period. I was reacting to her transferential hate and desires as well as to her defenses against these forces.

After about three years of treatment, Alicia tentatively suggested that the analysis was perhaps coming to its conclusion. I was thunderstruck. Fortunately, I behaved with restraint and expressed an interest in her thinking. She reminded me that she had been in therapy for about six years with an analytically oriented therapist before coming to see me. She felt our work had been vastly superior, and while she did not feel she had accomplished all she had hoped for, she was impressed with her gains and thought perhaps nine years of treatment was enough.

I was flabbergasted. This woman was ready to call her analysis completed with a somewhat satisfactory result while I could not be sure that we had even begun to analyze her. I still had no stable concept of the nature of our relationship. I also thought, with pained amusement, of how she would tell people in the community of her successful analysis with me, and I would have to listen silently to reports of a colossal fraud in which I was forced to collude through silence. Fortunately, she did not act on this urge to terminate.

When she made her shocking announcement, I reacted internally with an exaggerated version of my earlier experiences with her. I felt impotent and ignorant. If she had indeed traversed an entire analytic field, my own understanding lagged far behind hers. If she was terminating before movement was really underway, then I felt incapable of knowing even how to get an analysis started. I was experiencing a profound sense of loss of self. I realized that her early dissociative reactions and her typical emotionally isolated, intellectualized verbal behavior in the analysis had been triggering in me the same narcissistic vulnerability as now, although on a much less massive scale.

I regularly met Alicia's emotional inaccessibility with associations to my remote, laconic, and enigmatic father. As a child, I yearned deeply for communication from him. My memory tells me that although I strove for satisfying contact, I rarely achieved it. That old need was activated in Alicia's analysis. The central transforming issue for me with Alicia was that I brought my archaic search for my father's love to the encounter, and her remoteness inflamed my inner pain. This unconscious dynamic contributed greatly to our shared intersubjective field.

Although neither Alicia nor I regarded the other consciously as being like our parents, unconsciously we were engaged in a chronic effort to undo or eliminate parental coldness or ineffectuality. I probably withdrew consciously from her during much of the early period of the analysis, as I had consciously withdrawn from my emotionally unavailable father throughout much of my youth. Probably I began reacting unconsciously in a seeking mode soon after beginning Alicia's analysis.

I told her that she talked and moved as though she feared she might see, hear, touch, or smell something ugly or offensive. My impressions, conveyed to her in somewhat playful fashion, were part of a broader approach to her massive defenses against emotional contact and freedom, because such concrete, visual images were more difficult for her to isolate by intellectualization. My interpretation to her implicitly included an assurance that her dissociative defenses were not necessary in her relationship with me. I was neither the cold parent nor the invasive parent, and therefore she could "touch" me. I was thereby promising that we could "touch" each other and that such contact would be part of her experience of self-discovery, through tactile discovery of another person. This did not involve literal touching. I was aware through a dream of mine that urges to penetrate her life were active in me, but usually I had to struggle against not paying attention to her, a tendency stimulated in me by her intellectualized, remote verbalizations. She yearned for interpenetration and intimacy, but she did not know how to achieve it. I was also trying to ease the pain of my own longings for more complete parenting.

When Alicia proposed ending the analysis, I simply urged her to talk more about it. I assume, however, that those simple words must have conveyed to her that I did not agree with her suggestion. She then discussed the matter, and she gradually concluded that termination would be premature. She decided, however, that for an indefinite period she would sit, rather than lie, on the couch in order to intensify her experience of contact with me.

The quiet crisis in the analysis had now subsided, and I decided to tell her that her idea had enabled me to become acutely aware of how out of touch we continued to be. I was essentially informing her of my estimate of inordinate amounts of anxiety in our relationship. I believe I thus conveyed to her my agreement with her new postural policy. She even predicted that after she had gone through this more intense experience of me, she would be able to resume use of the couch, but with a new capability for symbolic intimacy.

As soon as she began to sit up on the couch, as though midway between plan and fate, or at the junction of interaction and abandon, she began a passionate effort to involve me in an erotic experience. It became a steamy, discomfiting time for me, as it should have been, because her past defensive, remote, self-reflectiveness had imposed a lulled, almost numbed effect on both of us. I now had little opportunity for thoughtful, subtle interpretations. My comments for the most part consisted of tactful refusals of sexual offerings.

The powerful interpretive subtext of my responses included two ideas: I was neither the distant mother (my visible distress indicated my intense impingement), nor was I the violating, unloving father (my refusal to invade her psychological space by counterseductiveness). Here we have another example of how multiple ideas of quite specific and pertinent nature—the essence of interpretation—are contained in and communicated by nonverbal behavior that superficially appears to be noninterpretive.

In contrast to her earlier distaste for touching living things, she was now intensely, almost frantically, seeking to make contact, to interpenetrate. The sexualized sitting up constituted a distinct phase of the analysis. Months later, when it ended, she resumed the couch. Never again did I have any basic doubt about her analytic contact with me. She had gone through the same remarkable experience as Adela Quested's in *A Passage to India:* "Although her hard schoolmistressy manner remained, she was no longer examining life, but being examined by it; she had become a real person" (Forster 1924).

Approximately two years later, we concluded the analysis by mutual decision and with a shared conviction that we had done curative, creative work.

8

INTERPRETATION DREAMS

The dynamic relationship of a dream and its interpretation bears important similarities to that of patient and therapist.* The dream and interpretation are reciprocally transforming. The study of this process contributes to a more comprehensive appreciation of the power and complexity of intersubjective events in psychotherapy.

This discussion will focus on certain dreams I call *interpretation dreams*. I define interpretation dreams as those dreams making generally reliable statements about the therapeutic process that the dreamer readily perceives without intervention by the analyst. An interpretation dream's powerful statement of meaning about the patient's life is readily evident to both the patient and the therapist. It may be a very simple dream, or it may be quite complex. Such dreams are prima facie evidence of the intimate connection of inter-

*Professor David James Fisher and Professor Robert Hill provided valuable consultation for this chapter.

pretation and dream. These dreams also give evidence of the connection between interpretation and the subjective experience of the patient at the level of unconscious fantasy. A thorough familiarity with the clinical characteristics of such dreams, the therapeutic circumstances in which they occur, and their influence on both dreamer and therapist enlarges the understanding of interpretation as a specific manifestation and a fundamental component of the therapeutic process.

Foucault (1984–1985) recognized the problem of the communicability of meaning in dreams. "In the realm of psychoanalytic investigation," he states, "the unity between a psychology of the image which demarcates the field of presence, and a psychology of meaning which defines the field of linguistic potentialities, has not been found. Psychoanalysis has never succeeded in making images speak" (p. 38). Foucault was not entirely correct. Indeed, there are analytic moments when dream images do speak. But of course, it depends on whether someone is there to listen.

Wittgenstein (1942–1946) approached the same problem as Foucault, but from the opposite direction. He wanted to know:

> Whether dreaming is a thought. Whether dreaming is thinking about something. . . . Suppose you look on a dream as a kind of language. A way of saying something, or a way of symbolizing something. . . . We might then find a way of translating this symbolism into the language of ordinary speech, ordinary thoughts. But then the translation ought to be possible both ways. It ought to be possible by employing the same technique to translate ordinary thoughts into dream language. As Freud recognizes, this never is done, and cannot be done. So we might question whether dreaming is a way of thinking something, whether it is a language at all. [p. 48]

From these comments, Foucault and Wittgenstein would appear to share Freud's (1900) skepticism about the manifest dream as an integral component of the human experience of discovery, problem solving, and communication. Freud's (1900) view of the relation of images and ideas in dreams is both intimidating and challenging. He stipulated categorically that the manifest dream had value only as a disguised expression of a repressed wish. He regarded a wish as a thought arising from a frustrated desire. However, Freud's wish fulfillment theory of dreams is no longer the dominant basis for understanding dream meanings. Rather, its present value resides more in its being a continuing reminder that we need to learn more about the ultimate psychological meaning of dreams.

Freud indirectly repudiated his own generalization about the emptiness of the manifest dream. In his approach to "typical" dreams, he said that dreams of nakedness, flying, falling, losing teeth, or taking examinations had certain general meanings that can be derived directly from the manifest contents, without the intervening necessity of the dreamer's free association. By attributing a consistent meaning to a particular manifest content, Freud was thus crediting the manifest content with a meaningful ideational substance.

Freud's (1900) *The Interpretation of Dreams* suggests a profoundly dialectical relationship between dreams and interpretations. In this work he invites the further exploration of the fundamental relationship between the two, including the possibility of discovery of interpretive potential in the manifest dream phenomena.

Wittgenstein (1942–1946) believes that the wish fulfillment theory itself is a general interpretation of dreams. He notes:

> It is characteristic of dreams that they often seem to the dreamer to call for an interpretation (p. 45).
>
> But dreams do seem to have something puzzling and in a special way interesting about them—so that we want an explanation of them (p. 45).

There seems to be something in dream images that has a certain resemblance to the signs of a language. As a series of marks on paper or sand might have (p. 45).

When a dream is interpreted we might say that it is fitted into a context in which it ceases to be puzzling. *In a sense the dreamer redreams his dream in surroundings such that its aspect changes* (italics mine) (p. 45).

To say that dreams are wish fulfillment is very important chiefly because it points to the sort of interpretation that is wanted—the sort of thing that would be an interpretation of a dream. As contrasted with an interpretation which said that dreams were simply memories of what happened, for instance (p. 47).

And some dreams obviously are wish fulfillments. . . (p. 47).

But it seems muddled to say that *all* dreams are hallucinated wish fulfillments (p. 47).

He (Freud) wanted to find some one explanation which would show what dreaming is. He wanted to find the *essence* of dreaming. And he would have rejected any suggestion that he might be partly right but not altogether so. If he was partly wrong, that would have meant that he was wrong altogether—that he had really not found the essence of dreaming (p. 48).

When he states that dreams seem to "*call* [italics mine] for an interpretation" (p. 45), Wittgenstein is attributing voice, and therefore thought, to the dream. And he specifies that the dream calls for an *interpretation* (italics mine)—not some other response. He seems to say that dream and interpretation each have a voice, and speak to one another. This belief seems related to Bakhtin's (1986) "doublevoicedness." The dialogue occurs between both dream and interpretation, dreamer and interpreter. There is also a counterpart dialogue occurring concomitantly within the dreamer (patient) and the interpreter (therapist). The interplay of image and meaning, and the inexorable creative consequence of it, is stated by Philip Roth: "The treacherous imagination is everybody's maker—we are all the invention of each other, everybody a conjuration conjuring up everyone else. We are all each other's authors" (*The Counterlife*, 1987, p. 164).

The basic relationship of dream and interpretation, then, consists of multiple dialogical processes, interpersonal and intrapsychic, intersubjective and intrasubjective. (The apposite overarching designation may be transubjectivity [Hill 1988].) This complex and appropriately unstable model requires "evenly hovering attention" and rapidly oscillating focalized attention occurring in fluent synchrony. Rycroft (1979) is a persuasive proponent of this newer approach. He states: "Dreams are not phenomena we observe but experiences we have and create for ourselves, and the appearance of objectivity is an illusion. . ." (p. 2). Rycroft attempts to erase the conventional distinctions between the objective and the subjective, the rational and the irrational, the literal and the symbolic, the analytic and the creative. He strives to reduce categorization and compartmentalization in our thinking about psychological life, including dreams. He opposes the strict assignment of function implied in Freud's (1900) wish fulfillment theory of dreams, in which expressive function is assigned to dreams, but an integrative, communicative, or creative capability is denied.

Traditional Freudian thinking insisted that symbolization was derived only from conflicted, repressed impulses. Current brain research has undermined such assumptions. Newer knowledge indicates that different kinds of brain activity produce different kinds of thinking. Recent neurophysiological studies, such as the work of Hobson (1988), have demonstrated that complex events from the brain stem to the cortex are involved in the production of dreams. Although different kinds of ideational processes occur, it is not possible to say that some are better or worse, richer or poorer, more advanced or more primitive, more free or more repressed than others. Primary process thinking is no longer to be connected, ipso facto, with unevolved, instinctual aspects of motivation and meaning.

Lacan (1978), in defying Freud's insistence on the turbulent anarchy of the unconscious with his famous assertion, "The unconscious (discovered by Freud) is structured in the most radical way like a language," helps to break down the distinction between a dream and its interpretation. By examining specifics of the complex dialogues about the dream occurring between and within the dreamer and the therapist, we are able to gain a more detailed understanding of both dreams and interpretations.

One might postulate that the subtext of a dream is an interpretation, and that the subtext of an interpretation likewise is a dream. If this assertion is correct, then dreams and interpretations, although seemingly polar opposites, enjoy a very important kinship, even a oneness as opposite sides of the same psychological coin.

The dream is experienced and expressed in a pictorial, imagic, nonverbal mode. Yet over and over again, the visual scene yields powerful ideas about meanings in the patient's life. Turgenev's famous comment that one picture is worth a thousand words at first seems to be a bit of self-mockery by the prolific author. However, looked at more carefully, it expresses the enormous density of ideas in visual images, and coincides with Freud's assertion that condensation is one of the main processes whereby dreams are formed. One dream image may compress many, if not a thousand, ideas.

What is the special consciousness of dreams and the relationship to the kind of consciousness reflected in and induced by interpretations? Clearly, one is pictorial while the other is verbal. Freud insisted that verbal ideas occurring in dreams did not represent verbal thought activity in the manifest dream itself. He also said the same thing about imagery in dreams. The dream, he believed, constitutes a defense which, properly read, reveals the inhering but disguised truth. Dream images, for Freud, are not active dialogical statements or components. He thought the dialogical aspects underlie the dream, motivate the dream's occurrence, and contribute sizably to the dream's overt characteristics. In a sense Freud converts verbal elements of manifest dreams to coequality with visual components. Verbal elements have the same dream function, according to Freud, as visual elements, but they are not identical.

In reducing words to pictures, Freud (1915) reversed the evolutionary order. First there was the idea of the thing (visual), then the idea of the word or name (verbal). This completed consciousness. But Freud converts wishes (or ideas) to pictures in manifest dreams, and in the analysis of dreams he proposes conversion of the pictures in the manifest dream to underlying wishes (ideas), thus implying a reciprocal process of words to pictures, pictures to words. Or, it might be restated, from the standpoint of intersubjectivity, dreams to interpretations, interpretations to dreams.

INTERPRETATION TO DREAM: THERAPIST

A 40-year-old man, an executive in the entertainment field, happily married, and the father of three small girls, had the following dream.

I am standing in a building, facing a wall consisting of drawers. An older man is there. He pulls open one of the drawers, and I realize this is like a morgue or mortuary. He shows me the remains of my father, lying on a slab, but most of the body is gone. The remains consist of organs, but little else. The man indicates that I should eat the body. He shows me an arm, he displays it as a butcher would. It resembles a tuna steak. I am revolted at the prospect of eating my father's body. I can't. The dream ends here.

Perhaps the dialectical relation of dream to the process of interpretation can best be stated by pointing out the immediate conscious difference in the dream's meaning for the patient and for me. He first experienced the dream as horrifying, frightening, disgusting, guilt-inducing, and saddening. For him, the imagery prevailed. On the other hand, I perceived and experienced and thought about the dream in terms of its meaning, its interpretation. However, this difference in initial response between us was not total. Listening noninterpretively, I also felt the horror of death when I first heard the dream—deaths in my family; concerns about my own mortality and that of loved ones; memories of other death experiences. But to the extent that I was hearing this dream as interpreter, these literal responses to the dream were not dominant.

The dream constituted a culmination and a challenge for us. Nothing like it had preceded it in our shared experience. It was a landmark, and its occurrence constituted an epiphanic moment, bringing a new richness and vitality to our dialogue.

This patient had begun his nonintensive analytically oriented therapy about two years earlier. At that time, he was struggling with a cocaine habit that was damaging his career and his marriage. When his wife finally announced that he had to choose between her and the cocaine, his internist referred him to me.

From the beginning of therapy, I was aware of his unusual psychological resources. He continued as he began, with a deceptively casual and informal—almost lazy—conversational style. He consistently seemed to abjure systematic development of any topic, but his conversation was always topical. Although his remarks frequently seemed indolent, almost aimless, he invariably was addressing an issue of great personal importance. And for some unexplained reason, he called me Joseph from the outset.

Although it was his problem with cocaine dependency that brought him to therapy, he was initially very concerned about his older sister, who had just been arrested in a southern city for seeking to obtain a narcotic by passing fake prescriptions at pharmacies. Because he had become like a distant, powerful father to his sister and several younger half-siblings, who were much less successful than he, he was also somewhat resentful and impatient. But it quickly became evident that the memories of his father's alcoholism and early death troubled him more profoundly than his sister's problems.

His parents had separated when he was about 2 years old, and his sister just a few years older. His father left his mother for another woman, whom he soon married, but the parents continued to live in the same area. The patient felt a profound loss of his father in the separation. Not too long thereafter the mother met and married another man with whom she had additional children. The patient's stepfather, unlike the father, was uneducated, authoritarian, cruel, and unsuccessful. The boy longed for love but received only toleration at best, punishment and rejection at worst. During the patient's puberty, his stepfather sexually molested his sister. When the patient's father learned of this, a near-scandal ensued, and his mother and stepfather fled, leaving the patient and his sister with the father. But several months later they regained custody of the patient and his sister and moved far away from the father, despite the father's best efforts to keep the children safely near him.

Throughout puberty and adolescence the absent father remained in the patient's mind as a loving, idealized figure who would rescue the patient from this cruel oblivion. The father had been a famous and creative celebrity who was ruined by a scandal. The father was also alcoholic, and he developed cirrhosis of the liver, with damage to his esophageal veins. The father's fortunes had not only failed, but he had narrowly escaped prosecution for alleged financial irregularities, and slipped into relative obscurity.

Nevertheless, the patient voluntarily rejoined his father in late adolescence, and felt that a long missing essential part of his life had finally been restored. He felt some guilt for leaving his relatively poor and unhappy mother, but this was outweighed by the presence of his beloved powerful father, who although financially impoverished, still seemed to the patient very richly endowed with symbolic strength.

The return to Eden lasted little more than one year. The father, despite severe liver disease, continued to drink heavily, and he died suddenly of hemorrhage of the varicose veins of the esophagus.

This abbreviated story of a life illustrates the prevalence of father issues and the paucity of mother themes. This patient has always been father-obsessed: with his beloved but absent good father, the hated and feared bad stepfather, and the employer whom the patient regarded with strong filial attitudes, and now the good father–therapist.

The patient's dream engendered many ideas in me:

1. Eating the father suggests oral incorporation, introjection, identification.

2. The scant remains suggested that the pickings are slim, so this is a father deficit that will always remain but must be made accessible in the therapy and faced rather than repressed.

3. I am probably the father, therefore, I am also of limited value to him, and this may be an attitude that the patient is reluctant to express.

4. The organs obviously were internal organs— this may represent the diseased liver and the bleeding esophagus; perhaps this means that we are still dealing with the acute traumatic effect upon the patient of the father's violent death.

5. The ingestion may have been symbolic of the cocaine habit, the problem that pushed the patient reluctantly into therapy.

All these ideas dealt with the major known developmental deficit: the lack of good fathering and the patient's deep incorporative hunger. They pointed to a deep and repressed oral dynamic. By the contrast of omission, they highlighted the mystery of the mother and suggested the hatred for the abandoning father and the sadistic stepfather. They accented the unresolved psychic trauma induced by the father's death and suggested the underlying psychodynamics of the cocaine habit.

The dream was mainly sheer agony for the patient. He saw and felt his father as a dead body, and he had to accept remnants as a substitute for a body. In addition, there was the ugly spectacle of the father's flesh being displayed as if in a butcher's shop. And finally there was the gruesome, horrifying prospect of having to eat the father. For the patient these were awful subjective experiences; they were not ideas. They were, to employ a paraphrase, the unbearable heaviness of being.

To help the patient transform these dreadful images into therapeutically valuable ideas, the therapist must oscillate between image and idea, between dream experience and interpretation. This statement suggests a deceptively simple process. Any therapist can attest that, while it is occurring, the process of finding the correct ideas in dreams is often painful, chaotic, and confusing.

How does the dreamer receive the ideas the therapist conveys? Ostensibly, the interpretation consists of words spoken by the therapist to the patient. But is that all the patient perceives? Superficially, the patient hears sounds that are immediately recognized as a group of words that express ideas. There are also paraverbal communications, such as tone of voice, facial expression, body tone and movement, which might actually contribute to a pictorial perception that is quite different from the manifest ideas contained in the spoken words, creating the possibility of a complicated and paradoxical situation. The patient reports a dream consisting of very painful images; underlying them are multiple frightening ideas potentially available to consciousness of which the dreamer is as yet unaware. The therapist is *relatively* less involved in these emotional issues and is therefore more able to translate the dream images into verbal ideas.

Yet the therapist may also have subjective responses to a patient's dreams. I can recall that this dream reactivated pictorial memories of my father's death and the deaths of other family members, as well as thoughts of my own death. This subjective response ought not to be viewed as an interference, for personal images are important ingredients in the production of the verbal ideas that can eventually be imparted to the patient. However, when the therapist's situation is compared with that of the patient, it seems relatively placid. The calmly stated words of the therapist can be and often are highly inflammatory for the patient, who may cry, recoil, become enraged, or feel panic. The therapist's ideas are almost always instantly transformed by the patient into images, the nature of which is disclosed by the patient's attendant affect. As Wittgenstein (1942–1946) has noted, the process of interpretation causes the patient to redream the dream. Or the interpretation is transformed into dream. Once again, the powerful and inseparable intimacy of dream image to interpretation becomes lived out.

Another way to look at the issue is that the dream images are expressions of the nondiscursive, symbolic forms of thought characteristic of the nondominant hemisphere of the brain. The degree of decoding required to understand dream symbols will depend not only upon the complexity of the symbol, but also upon the familiarity of the therapist with dreams and with symbolism in general. So if dream and interpretation are different forms of thought, it becomes easier to appreciate that a dream image and a dream interpretation are highly interpenetrative. Nevertheless, they are not identical—a symbol remains a symbol, and an interpretation is always an interpretation. However, there is a shared, submerged aspect of each in the other. Ideas underlie dream images, and dreamlike images underlie interpretations. They are two sides of the same coin. They are alike and also different. They oppose, inform, and shape one another.

The universal human tendency to see not only printed letters, words, numbers, and sentences, but also simultaneously to perceive pictures or images in these very same entities further illustrates this relationship, which can be described as the glyphic function of reading. The less familiar the letters, the more the pictorial quality is noticed. For example, looking at Chinese characters, non-Chinese speakers are especially aware of the visual aspects: the density of the print, the curves and angles of the letters, and the relations of the visible parts to one another. On the other hand, when reading English, English speakers are generally less aware of the pictorial curvature of the letters—their attention is focused on the meanings, the ideas that the letters and words express. All written languages are essentially glyphic. The more exotic the script, the more evident will be the pictorial properties to the viewer.

Dreams are like Egyptian hieroglyphics, a verbal–pictorial mode of communicating ideas. The person with the greatest understanding of dreams as language will be the most capable of discerning the ideas expressed in the dream images, that is, will be the most literate, the most able to read the dream language. Ideally, this experience and skill should be possessed by psychotherapists. As the therapist progresses in understanding a dream, its ideational meaning gradually supersedes and supplants its graphic significance. In other words, the pictorial, artistic quality of the dream diminishes as understanding grows, yet the total experience—pictorial and interpretive—becomes richer and more vivid.

DREAM TO INTERPRETATION: DREAMER

Because of the plasticity of dreams it is possible to observe change in a person who is a character in a dream while a dream is occurring. When such transformations occur, meaning that previously has been shrouded can become visible, and then important changes may occur in the life of the dreamer. When the dreamer has the awesome experience of seeing a person become someone else, he observes the change, and it becomes an unforgettable demonstration of the crucial linkage in the dreamer's mind between two other vitally important and conflict-laden people. It also shows the deconstruction of that same connection. The following examples illustrate the vividness and power of this experience.

On the eve of a separation from his wife, a man in his middle forties dreamed that he was gazing at his beautiful wife. As he watched, she became unattractive and, to his surprise, her face became his mother's face. In therapy, this patient's two chief complaints had been his mother's basic coldness and his wife's indifference to him. Early in his therapy, he cried a great deal and hoped that through his perseverance and fidelity, his wife would become loving and faithful. However, as therapy progressed, he became aware that his yearnings toward his wife were heavily influenced by vain hopes for his mother's love, and he was gradually liberated from the painful neediness directed to these two women, neither of whom would or could meet his needs. The events of the dream convinced him that his wife and his mother had the same unconscious meaning, and the active transformation of one face into another seems to reflect his increased active mastery of his life difficulties. This dream, occurring as his divorce became imminent, consolidated his insight into the connection between his past and his present and symbolized his readiness to meet a momentous life change. The patient's dream was, in other words, the interpretation.

In another dream, a 51-year-old dreamer stands in front of a thick oak door. She opens the door and sees her sick father, who looks awful. She asks why he hasn't told her and her younger sister that he is still alive. He replies that he has his own life to lead. Feeling hurt, she begins to cry. Then he tells her that he has two more daughters, and she sees the two little girls. She becomes furious with him—with a quality and intensity of anger that she had never felt before. As all this happens, the patient's father's hair becomes dark brown, and her father is now her husband.

Before the dream, this woman had been in weekly psychotherapy for approximately one year. She wanted therapy because of a difficulty in achieving orgasm. She and I quickly established a friendly, collaborative relationship. She knew, and her husband knew, that she was excessively nice in their relationship and unable to express the underlying anger she felt toward him. The husband and wife both realized that her pattern of relating to important men derived from her experiences with her father, who became fatally ill during the patient's puberty and died when she was an older adolescent. During her father's illness, she became the anchor and caretaker of the family.

When I pointed out to the patient her use of manifold altruistic traits as defense against her unacceptable anger, she received my interpretations with good humor and intellectual acceptance. But she didn't internalize this interpretation until she had the dream in which her blond father turned into her brunette husband. Now she could "feel" her anger toward her husband.

It is interesting to note that the patient believed that she discerned in me some of the same personality traits that she possessed. When her loved ones had pointed out her submerged anger, she felt accused, but because she identified with me, she was able to accept my interpretations with more ease. Prior to her dream, she and I had already done considerable work on the presumptive anger stemming from her adolescence. We agreed that her father's illness and death had stolen much of her youth and propelled her into premature adulthood. The lesson of these events was that she did not have the luxury of expressing her angry emotions. In the weeks before this dream, however, the patient had become somewhat more aware of anger toward her father and more alert to a variety of frustrated feelings toward her husband. But these insights had remained insecure, and she had not experienced the fundamental unity of father–husband anger until the dream. It consolidated her understanding of her salient life problems in a much more powerful way than my interpretation alone could induce.

These two dreams are striking both in their similarities and their differences. Each literally shows the unconscious equation of mate and parent. When the wife became the hated mother, it was coincident with dissolution of the marriage. But when the father turned into the loved husband, the marital relation improved.

These dreams exemplify a category of dreams that may legitimately be termed interpretation dreams. They show that to the dreamer, two different characters in the dream are equated, and they also predict an outcome by the direction of the transformation, and this insight occurs *spontaneously* with recall of the dream. Verbal explication of the dream ideas would, of course, add detail, texture, and discursive linkage, but powerful interpretations inhere in the dreams themselves and in their recall.

In this class of dream, the subjective experiences of both dreamer and therapist are more alike than in the dream about the dead father. That dream was comprised of horrifying images for the dreamer, while the analyst experienced mainly psychological formulations. The dreams about mates and parents were qualitatively different from the father dream in that one important person became another. They were also the dreams of patients who had developed greater skill and confidence in self-analysis. As analytic and therapeutic progress occurs, dreams achieve greater interpretive quality.

Although the focus of this discussion has been upon the dream and its interpretive quality, or lack of same, these important phenomena occurred within the overarching, comprehensive intersubjective process shared by patient and analyst. The impression that interpretation dreams are discrete, clearly definable entities must be tempered by a simultaneous appreciation that these dreams can occur only as components of the more complete intersubjective field of action.

The process whereby dreams generate interpretations and interpretations induce new dreams can be further elucidated. Phenomenologically, *interpretation* dreams are transformational. The dream of the scant remains of the dead father is, significantly, nontransformational. And it was not an interpretation dream; rather, it helped prepare the patient for interpretation. On the other hand, the dream of a transformation of wife into mother or of father into husband occurs in the interpretation dreams. This is the surface manifestation of a profound and powerful fluidity through which interpretations cause a redreaming of the dream and the dream reinterprets the interpretation. The reversal of parent into mate or vice versa in the dream informs both dreamer and therapist that the dream has produced a culminating interpretation, consolidating the awareness of the displacement, an awareness that has been growing through the ongoing interpretive process. The inversion of parent and mate also indicates a higher interpretive level than that achieved by the displacement interpretations made prior to the dream.

Interpretations are not only intersubjective, they are also intrasubjective, being generated through one's own dream. Following Bahktin's (1986) principle that all understanding is dialogical, the new interpretation arising within one's own dream is also intersubjective as well as intrasubjective, resulting as it does from the dialogue between different voices within oneself.

Here we have another situation in which interpretation and intersubjectivity are seen to be inseparable. We analysts generate interpretations from our own dream lives, thereby relying heavily upon our own subjectivity to interpret the other person's subjective experience.

9

INTERPRETATION: SELF-CENTERED INTERVENTION

Self has become the transcending concept of psychoanalysis and dynamic psychotherapy. The new school of self psychology, established by Kohut (1977), is the most dramatic sign of the centrality of self-centered intervention. The emphasis on self is probably Kohut's most powerful contribution.

Self, however, is an untidy concept. Its meanings often seem as numerous as its users. Every psychotherapeutic interpretation is basically referential to the self. But this was not adequately appreciated until "self" achieved a more prominent and clear position in psychodynamic theory.

The self of the patient is not the only self referent; each interpretation derives from, and influences, the self of the therapist as well. No matter what overt form an interpretation takes, it is invariably an expression of the life of the self, of both therapist and patient, and it is at the same time the most immediate reflection of the changing reality resulting from the encounter of the two selves.

Interpretations now, as before, produce insight, make conscious that which was unconscious, reduce the dominance of superego, shift the balance between defense and impulse. But these effects must always be correlated with the evolution of self that should be occurring. The primary focus and influence of interpretation are upon the self.

Psychotherapists have been understandably reluctant to make the self the centerpiece of psychodynamic thought and practice. The notion of self, with its uncertainties, carries some uncomfortably heavy baggage. Self, for example, can discomfitingly overlap soul, with its metaphysical implications. Therefore, a therapist who employs self as a central factor in human experience must accept the possible presence of some element of the metaphysical in his or her thinking. Freud's solutions was to adhere to a machinelike model of the human psyche driven by a power source called instincts. But this aggravates the problem instead of solving it. Psychological events need to be analyzed in humanistic, existential, and experiential terms.

Freud's (1900) machine analogy makes this task more difficult. The concept of self as the dynamic center can have very little status in a psychoanalytic theory based upon physicochemical analogies. Yet Freud was not consistent in this mechanistic bias—for instance, Bettelheim (1983) contends that Freud's original German is less mechanistic in content and tone than are the English translations. Moreover, Freud's writings are replete with implicit humanistic assumptions that cannot validly be subsumed into a mechanistic model.

Furthermore, the use of the language of physical science does not eliminate the metaphysical potential in psychological discourse. For instance, even if it is assumed that a human psyche emerges from an original id, an inchoate flux of instinctual urges, the same wearisome questions may still arise. What created this id, and to what end? Does the id have an existence of its own, and is it subject to the same possible reincarnating transubstantiation as a soul or a self? These are the same metaphysical questions that present themselves when human experience is considered from the standpoint of self. The language of mechanics does not eliminate the possibility of such speculation.

Among current writers, Schafer's (1983) emphasis on the patient as agent, rather than as object, is extremely relevant. He sees analysis as a human transaction, and insists the analytic process should be discussed and thought about in human terms, rather than in the language of physical science. Self as agent possesses much more cogency for the human experience than reference to libidinal drive. Self is central for motivation, action, organization, and reflection. Nothing can be more human than attention to self. Hence, the justification for primacy of self in psychoanalytic and psychotherapeutic discourse.

Existence and experience: these are the fundamental components of self. The appropriation of a ruthless materialism denies any special a priori meaning to an individual's existence, but this very abolition establishes the precondition for the creation of meaning through a person's involvement in life. The self arises only from this life and its evolving experiences and relationships. Meaning and meanings are inevitable concomitants of these events. This is a firmly humanistic perspective.

The leading position of self, then, implies the prime importance of active selves interacting, and intersubjectivity becomes a basic experiential principle. Developmentally, the intersubjective understanding of the family means the involvement of the self of the mother (as well as the father) and the self of the child. The total psychological experience of each party interacts with the other through the respective self of each. The same principle applies to the psychotherapeutic process.

Winnicott (1965) perceived such issues with exceptional

clarity. His concepts of the holding environment, good enough mothering, and transitional phenomena are brilliant manifestations of this understanding. Winnicott powerfully illustrates the poignant conjunction of oneness and separateness of mother and child. The mother who shows the child through living example that the child can kill the mother (in fantasy and symbolic action) and yet that the mother, as well as her affection for the child, can survive undamaged, is enabling the child to believe that his or her own aggression is a nonlethal resource that can be accepted and utilized as a force for creative living. Otherwise, the child will handle aggression by repression, disavowal, rationalization, or some other defense in order to split the aggression off from the self, thus creating a false self. The mother who is true to herself (unafraid of her own aggression, unafraid of her child's aggression) can teach her child to love and develop his own true self.

The true self is all of the self with its disparate and frightening elements. Sequestration or disavowal of any aspect of self inevitably establishes the false self. That which the child hides from his mother (and father), and the rest of the world, reduces self. False self is essentially reduced self.

Stripped of its elaborations, Kohut's (1977) theory of self disorder may be regarded as directly derived from Winnicott's false self. Kohut emphasizes that the healthy self is a full self. Mirroring, idealizing, and twinning experiences from self objects must be sufficiently abundant or a deficit of self exists, and the person evolves with a fragmented, noncohesive, immature self, fruitlessly seeking fulfillment of unmet self needs.

Qualitative and quantitative requirements must be met in Kohut's theory of the self. If these requirements go unmet, self disturbance ensues. The unmet needs distort both the self and all subsequent self-object relationships. Kohut and his associates have delineated the defensive consequences of unmet self needs. The true self here consists of the largely concealed unmet needs, and the false self is the manifest self, which is mainly defensive.

Kohut's mature, bipolar self is an interesting and useful restatement or extension of Winnicott's true self. This is the self of contemporary psychodynamic interest. It is the self that can be observed, sensed, or intuited by the other; it is not a self that has been metapsychologically or metaphysically derived. It is a self that initially arises from the intensely intersubjective mother–child unity, and it continues to develop throughout life in the interpersonal, intersubjective human environment. Self and identity are interpenetrating concepts. Lichtenstein (1977) pointed out that no person's identity can ever be taken for granted, and assumed to be fully developed and stable. Instead, it is always in flux, evolving, even endangered. The self partakes of the same dynamic properties, enjoys the same challenges, and endures the same risks.

Why is self crucial for an optimal comprehension of interpretation? Interpretation cannot be validly conceived as other than an exquisitely intimate and momentary and immediate phenomenon. The attempt to purify or intellectualize the meaning of interpretation fails because such an effort deprives interpretation of its intimate essence. The interpretation reflects and comments on a passionate intersubjective moment; it is also a pulsating part of that moment. The interpretation arises from unconscious experience and addresses consciousness; interpretation and interpreter are one. The receiving consciousness of the patient reacts to, and influences, the interpretation and interpreter, with significant effect on the inner life of the interpreter.

Traditional psychoanalytic theory inclines toward depersonalizing the interpreter, and this tendency impairs the understanding of interpretation. The person and the humanness of the interpreter must be included in the definition of the interpreter, and here the notion of self becomes critical. A similar circumstance exists with respect to the patient. While much of an interpretation may address the unconscious zone of the psychological life of the patient, the interpretation per se is offered to a person.

The therapist's capacity to conceive at all times that a coherent, cohesive self is potentially present and available in the analysand may be his or her most potent resource. Even the most disorganized, disturbed patient must be presumed to be expressing an organized self, however obscure and elusive that self may be for the analyst. If such a self cannot be discovered, the analyst's conviction and effort contribute to the achievement of such a therapeutic self.

An interpretation may be very carefully formulated in order to focus specifically on an unconscious dynamic, but unless it is knowingly delivered to a person with a self, it is not an effective interpretation. When the therapist continuously has the patient as self as the primary focus, the necessary condition obtains. Increased self-awareness of the therapist always attends consciousness of the patient's self. An interpretation addressed to a self has several powerful effects: the interpretation increases the intimate linkage of therapist and patient; the patient perceives the personal, rather than impersonal, intentions of the interpreter (and interpretation); the most immediately important self needs are met; and simultaneously, the interpretation expresses and influences the therapist's self.

A productive therapeutic experience invariably is linked to a "meeting of minds," which really means a meeting of selves. Therapy fails when a union of selves is not achieved. When patient and therapist meet one another with well-established selves, they interact productively. Many psychotherapists have developed this self-seeking skill without conscious recognition. With the addition of conscious awareness, the therapist's effectiveness and enjoyment is significantly increased. Every psychodynamic interpretation is about the self and involves interacting selves. Clarke and Holquist (1984) report: "The Bakhtinian self is never whole, since it can only exist dialogically. It is not a substance or essence in its own right but exists only in a tensile relationship with all that is other and, most important, with other selves" (p. 65).

In the following case, emphasis upon the self, and self-based interpretations, were especially conspicuous throughout the therapy. It illustrates the value of focus on self.

W. C., a 33-year-old male writer, entered psychotherapy because of depression he consciously ascribed to his inability to establish himself as a professional television and screen writer. He was happily married, and at the beginning of his therapy, his wife was pregnant for the first time. The patient had been in treatment with an experienced female therapist for several years. While they felt his therapy was initially productive, they sensed that it had lost its momentum. Hence his therapist referred him to me with the explicit message that he was blocked in his career development by his internal relationship to himself and his family, that he was one of those young people who are actually handicapped by being wealthy through inheritance, and that he needed a suitable father-figure therapist in order to resume his psychological development.

At our first meeting I sensed that he suffered from a serious self disturbance. My powerful experience was of a person who was incomplete. He was obviously intelligent, sensitive, thoughtful, and creative. But in some hard-to-describe way, a spark—or something—was missing. The promising parts of him did not seem to come together in a way that generated interest, pleasure, and action in our encounters. My immediate formulation was a self disturbance, and this proved to be an exceedingly useful initial set.

The patient told me that he felt a need for more therapy because he was still unable to establish himself as a writer.

He was sure that the professional difficulties were in part due to his unresolved psychological problems. He was tall, thin, and boyish. He seemed sensitive and vulnerable and frightened. He made himself talk, but his speech had a quality of helpless defiance and reproach, and he was consciously resentful of having to see and talk to me. He appeared to be very concerned about being hurt. Although he knew that he needed more assistance and that he had been helped by his previous therapist, he also felt somewhat let down that she had not accomplished more. He feared that I too would disappoint him.

He was the third of four siblings, with two older brothers and a younger sister. He conveyed the impression that his parents had had a conventional and happy marriage. His father had died of a stroke a couple of years earlier.

When the patient was born, the father was beginning his ascent to wealth and power. From the dawn of his consciousness, the patient had felt that he was his mother's possession. By contrast, he perceived his two older brothers as exempt from her ownership. His mother doted on him, discouraged him from being involved in rougher sports and play, and encouraged artistic and aesthetic interests. She thought he was beautiful. She called him a "doll." Needless to say, his mother's attitude both pleased and displeased him. Like a doll, he believed he lacked physical strength; rough games and physical contact frightened him. He was a good student but he was shy and insecure.

His brothers, as he recalls them, were impatient, critical, and disdainful toward him. His father displayed the same unpleasant attitudes. He yearned particularly for love and approval from his father, and he believed he never received it. His father's gruff disapproval terrified him. The patient experienced the same longing and fears toward his brothers, but to a lesser degree.

I felt an acute sense of not being given to, of no vital input coming to me, of no stimulation or satisfaction. These immediate experiences alerted me to the self problem and to the probability that my feelings mirrored the patient's feelings. His appropriate male self needs had obviously been unmet through most of his life, and he had developed a sulky, hypersensitive, somewhat neutered false self. Fortunately, he was also aware of all this. Nevertheless, his immediate effect upon me was the evocation of feelings of mild depression and dysphoria. My awareness of my specific subjective response to him enabled me consciously to define his inner experience of self starvation. I silently organized these thoughts. This process activated my interest in him, and I was able to develop a vigorous, intense stance toward him, which was the key behavior responsive to his powerful unmet needs. I reviewed with him and focused upon his history of very unsatisfactory mirroring experiences with his parents and the consequent distortions of self development. My total set of attitudes and behaviors with this person concentrated around questions of self: his sense of being a doll, engendered by his mother, his castrated sense of self, resulting from the negative mirroring experiences with his father and older brothers, the derivative expressions of these earlier events on his shaky identity as a writer, and the looming problems stimulated by his wife's pregnancy and the imminence of parenthood.

All these self foci occurred during the first months of the therapy. I quite consciously maintained an affirming, filling attitude toward the patient. My interpretations were that he felt great anguish and deprivation because neither parent had been aware that he wanted to be a strong, self-reliant boy who also happened to be sensitive and aesthetically talented. His younger sister always demonstrated an affirming attitude toward him. Since she was the baby and female in a patriarchal and mainly authoritarian family, her ability to help him was limited.

The patient responded with enthusiasm to my accent on mirroring. He expressed to me that he felt understood and helped in a new way, that a spark existed in this therapy that energized him. From this point on, he felt sustained feelings of fondness toward me.

He now felt reinforced in his ambition to become a

successful writer, and on this basis he made a difficult decision to reject a profitable career opportunity as a technical writer and editor with attractive potential business opportunities. His wife, an aspiring artist, supported him in this decision.

Together we elucidated and defined a number of false selves that contributed to his identity diffusion and retardation. He perceived himself to be a doll, without energy, strength, or will. Another false self perception was as a frightened, sissified boy–girl. The first distorted self view conformed to his mother's neurotic need, and the second to his father's. He also defined himself as an unpleasant, inept kid whose presence was annoying to others—a reflection of his older brothers' resentfully rivalrous devaluation of him.

My own early concern with being a frightened sissy or a maladroit, unlovable kid brother was evident to me in the course of our therapeutic work. This awareness enabled me to maintain a sympathetic feeling of identification with him. I assumed that I conveyed this experience of mine to him through subtextual processes. Furthermore, I suspect that we conjoined in our shared unconscious striving for self authenticity, and the abolition of our respective false selves.

Another important self-oriented interpretation concerned the patient's feeling about his childhood and adolescence as a vacuous, aimless, endless drift. He had lacked a satisfying sense of himself and the world about him. I pointed out that this also was an aspect of a false self, a kind of negative self, obscuring important self-defining processes that were occurring beneath a deceptively dull surface. Multiple suicides in his peer group in late adolescence, including those of two close male friends, rendered the patient's growing anxiety and despair more actively available to him. From that time, a growing consciousness of self and self definition developed. My conscious focus, my interpretive content, and my more personal, intimate associations throughout the eight-month period dealt mainly with issues of self.

This man's literary specialty is absurdist screenplays and novels. In a comic mode, he chronicles the many mishaps that can occur on a journey on the path to meaning. Obviously, the singularity of his personal struggle reflects universals, and this capability engages the receptive analyst in an intense intersubjective process of self definition. As this process developed, I became more able to identify with the universal aspects of his experiences and, from this, to continue my personal self exploration, which then fed back into the therapeutic transactions.

Although diverse self issues developed, the prime accomplishment for the patient was the reclamation and further development of his positive identification with his father. He perceived that behind the father's gruff impatience with the patient's passive and unassertive stance was disappointment and a yearning for the patient to develop the resources the father sensed in him. He also became aware that the mother's protectiveness and comfort had the powerful effect of discouraging his differentiation and autonomy. With the clarification of these matters, he has enjoyed a powerful burst of self definition and actualization that is evident in all the important spheres of his life. Conscious and unconscious interest in the issue of self on both our parts has been a powerful influence on this process.

This psychoanalytic psychotherapy extended over several years. Approximately two years before termination the patient and his wife had their first child, a boy. The patient became exquisitely attuned to his baby's self needs, to the benefit of his son's development. His consciousness of self was also a powerful catalyst in the patient's continued psychological transformations.

The patient persisted in his writing efforts despite a continuing lack of recognition. His ability to persevere was itself evidence of his enhanced self-esteem. He now resolved that he would terminate treatment when he sold his first teleplay or screen play. One year later, he sold a script to one of the most popular and critically acclaimed television shows. Shortly thereafter, he did terminate his work with me. Six months later he returned, as scheduled, for a follow-up visit. He reported the birth of a little girl. Also, he had become a story editor on a major new weekly television show. This choice position, achieved by a small number of television writers, symbolized an enormous self-actualization attainment by the patient. He integrated these developmental achievements effectively. Mature self-esteem prevailed, while sulky self-doubt vanished.

The patient attributed much of his life enrichment to his experience in therapy and specifically to the therapeutic focus on issues of self. The therapist who helps a patient achieve phase-appropriate self-definition invariably accomplishes a counterpart task of his or her own, even if unaware of the ongoing inner change.

10

INTERPRETATION AND THE THERAPIST

Conventional reports of the psychodynamic development of an interpretive communication usually exclude the subjective experience of the therapist, which may have embarrassing and inconvenient features. Nevertheless, these unconventional phenomena are part of the process that produces the interpretation, and to omit discussion of these relevant experiences diminishes the accuracy of the presentation. Most of these do not render the therapist vulnerable to criticism, real or imagined. Many intimate memories and dynamics may be neither painful nor exciting to disclose, nor stimulating or offensive to read. However, the disclosure of certain other intrapsychic matters may not only be uncomfortable for the writer, but may also be regarded as unseemly and inappropriate by the reader. The omission of such inconvenient data may seriously reduce the truth value of the presentation.

THE THERAPIST'S PSYCHOLOGICAL ROLE
IN INTERPRETATION

To delete the embarrassing, the petty, and the unsavory from the therapist's account of his or her inner experience may well do some violence to a complete understanding of the interpretation. Sartre (as reported in Contat 1975) stated that while transparency is ultimately desirable in human affairs, the savage nature of contemporary social relations renders this desideratum impractical in most situations, with serious loss to all parties. The frequent practical necessity for selective omission impairs the quality of intrapsychic and interpersonal life. Therefore, if the choice in human relations is thus reduced to vulnerability versus falsification, the former should be much preferred. The same principle applies to discussions of the dynamics of the therapeutic process and the development of interpretation.

Because it involves all aspects of a relationship between two people, such as intense emotions, questions of values and morals, and other unconscious psychological factors, interpretation addresses the whole person of the patient, and the psychological world he or she inhabits. And it draws from the counterparts in the therapist. Effective understanding of this exquisitely human experience requires involvement of the whole person of the therapist. The adoption of this approach by the therapist inexorably, and usually implicitly, conveys to the patient that all aspects of a person's life are enriched by exploration of a wide range of intersubjective experiences. As a result, the patient more exuberantly faces his or her intricate and contradictory feelings, images, and wishes. After all, the therapist has, in an essential way, communicated that he or she is continuously in the same kind of experience as the patient—and so is everyone.

If it becomes commonly accepted knowledge that the inner life of the therapist is an integral part of the therapeutic process, supervisors will no longer ask supervisees, "Were you having some fantasy [of a personal nature] at that moment?" Instead, the apposite inquiry would be, "What was the fantasy you were having, and how do you think it influenced the therapeutic process?"

OPTIMAL THERAPIST SELF-SCRUTINY IN THE THERAPEUTIC SITUATION

To achieve their interpretive goals, therapists must monitor their ongoing involvement in the therapeutic process. Inattention to their own inner lives drastically diminishes interpretive possibilities.

Analytic orientation to therapy necessitates that the therapist scan his or her inner horizons throughout the therapeutic experience in a spontaneous, free-associative, non-programmatic way. Yet the usual psychodynamic assertions suggest discrete moments, often quite dramatic, in which the therapist perceives with some surprise how he has had a distorting influence on the therapeutic process, of which his own psychological preoccupations have hitherto rendered him unaware. Such epiphanic moments may occur frequently, influentially, and instructively.

The unfortunate tendency to limit attention to therapists' emotions primarily to these sensational but sporadic circumstances is congruent with the "countertransference" theory of therapist involvement. In effect, it advises: when excessive discomfort or disorder arises in psychotherapy, or when crisis looms, then it becomes propitious for the therapist to look inward. A corollary consequence is the relative neglect of the therapist's psychological experiences during the intercritical periods. Eventually, this neglect becomes policy. And ultimately it achieves a theoretical status: countertransference achieves importance during periods of unusual therapeutic intensity; otherwise the therapist's subjectivity is inactive or insignificant. This is a false and misleading assumption.

Recently, a supervisee asked how and when the therapist should decide to follow his own reactions. This important question is impossible to answer in a consistent way because self-attunement by the therapist cannot be based upon formal rules, guidelines, or theoretical strictures. Instead, here are a series of thoughts and clinical anecdotes that may illuminate the matter.

The first and guiding requirement is for the therapist to recognize that a quintessentially personal involvement develops between patient and therapist. The therapist, then, should develop a method of achieving and maintaining continuous effective contact with his or her own subjective experience of the therapy.

Many years ago, a married woman came to me for therapy. She saw me for a brief period, and she found the experience somewhat helpful. What I recall most vividly is that she resembled my eldest sister in physical appearance and personality. I became aware that our conversations were, for me, filtered through a screen of sisterly subjectivity. I doubted that this quality of my experience impaired the therapy. I had the feeling that it probably enriched the therapy, but I could not specify how it was helpful, except that I was certain that my essential impingement on her was thus intensified and that her psychological involvement with the therapy was correspondingly increased. These early professional experiences helped me develop a sensitivity to intersubjective considerations.

This event consolidated other experiences of the same type; for example, another patient reminded me of another sister, who was three years my senior. To me, this sister was the crying baby requiring comfort, yet she was also a cranky critic with power over me due to the erotic sibling bond.

When I noted my distinct sibling reactions to these patients, I began to classify each new patient as one of my siblings or parents. Since I am the youngest of a family of seven, consisting of parents and four older sisters, I had been favored with a fairly broad range of individuals who constitute my basic universe of personality variations. With time, it became possible to perceive combinations of more than one family member in the same patient. I also realize retrospectively that I tended not to include myself as one of the family types. Since patients invariably evoke strong feelings in me, this method of quickly establishing the familial/emotional relevance of a new patient permitted me a more rapid and clear consciousness of the countertransference evocations during the early transactions with a patient. My somewhat naïve and awkward method expressed a developing awareness that the therapist's emotional life is an essential component of the therapeutic process. This, I propose, is the transcendent concept. It should subordinate and subsume countertransference.

But, the thoughtful and persistent student should further inquire, if the therapist spends so much time thinking about and reacting to himself, could he thereby neglect his patients' needs? Or what is the optimum of attention (in terms of time and intensity) the therapist should consciously give to the patient, and what to himself?

These questions possess obvious commonsense importance. Therapy that neglects the patient becomes an absurdity. Furthermore, a therapist should not live like a tightrope walker who maintains a delicate balance in a state of high tension between the ever-present hazards of falling deep into his own feelings or completely losing awareness of his own emotions. Freud's (1912) dictum regarding free-floating, evenly hovering attention remains the best antidote to a mechanistic or formulaic approach to the management of the therapist's attention. Adherence in practice to this principle enables the learning therapist to gain a confident mastery of the silent dimension of therapist activity. The question of "how much" to each area will lose its rigidity, and the answer, "as much as necessary," will seem less like a Delphic evasion.

But here we must also ask about the hazards of emphasizing the analyst's subjective involvement in the therapeutic experience. Do analysts overidentify with patients? Do analytic relationships sometimes lose their professional validity and exist primarily to gratify personal needs of the therapist? Can boundaries between therapist and patient become so obscure or faint that therapeutic potential is destroyed? The answer to all these questions is a regretful "yes." But paradoxically the more ample the therapist's awareness of his or her subjective experience and its extended meanings, the less the likelihood of destructive developments. This awareness will enable the therapist to know when to become carefully quiet, when to cancel an appointment, or even when to transfer a patient to another therapist.

In my experience, any subjective elements of the therapist, no matter how extreme or unconventional, *can* constitute valuable input. The outcome depends on how the therapist processes his or her fantasies and feelings. It has become a virtual commonplace in psychoanalysis and psychotherapeutic discussions to point out that hostile or erotic impulses in the therapist can be turned to therapeutic advantage. Winnicott (1958), for example, showed that the analyst's hatred of the patient can constitute an ultimately constructive influence on the treatment.

The achievement of optimal utilization of the analyst's subjective responses is greatly facilitated by a two-stage approach to interpretation. The violent emotions of the therapist become harmful if they invade the work of the second stage, rather than becoming accessible as the raw material for the second stage. In fact, some of the therapist's most painful experiences with a patient can produce the most powerfully transmuting effects, if they are handled undefensively by the therapist. The following excerpts from the treatment of an academic sociologist may illustrate some of these points.

The patient was in her late thirties, married, and with two children. She immersed herself in treatment with tremendous intensity and total conscious candor. She needed help for both depression and some anxiety symptoms of hysterical form. These were associated with a major restiveness in her marriage.

Her therapeutic attention often focused on early childhood, but this invariably became permeated with a sense of disloyalty to her family, culminating in an indescribably "horrible" feeling. This first year of the analysis was also punctuated by horrible feelings about me, in which she felt that I would disrupt our usual empathic resonance with some egregious "helpful" comment she did not request and did not want. She experienced these as infuriatingly violative and disappointing.

While I regularly acknowledged to her my insensitive behavior, I also felt very hurt by the magnitude of her outraged feelings toward me. Had I chosen to justify myself by insisting that she was falsifying the meaning of my act or by dwelling on her overreaction, I would have been engaging in a defensive interpretation that would have been antitherapeutic. This would be an example of how the raw emotions would have invaded the second stage—that is, the stage of conscious, formal construction of the interpretations. I would not have been pursuing her psychological truths; instead I would have been trying to protect myself from hurt feelings and their real meanings. She was terribly hurt; I was very hurt by her. Had I defended myself internally and interpersonally, this would have constituted overidentification and, at its worst, could have destroyed the analysis. By employing my painful identification with her as a stimulus for self study,

I converted the experience into an event of great importance for the analysis.

Later in the analysis, as I became more fluent in our transactions, her violently painful responses to me withered away. Concomitantly, she began to recover memories from age 3 to 4 years of repeated sexual molestation by her father. This crucial childhood trauma became the central focus of the analysis. We could now interpret her terrible feelings of being violated by me as transferential reliving of her experience of being sexually exploited by her father and also being used by her unhappily married mother. Her mother was indirectly complicitous in the sexual abuse by neglecting her maternal responsibilities to the patient and thus providing the emotionally irresponsible father with ample opportunity. Her early hyperprotective, "loyal" feelings to her parents diminished as she gained these insights.

Perhaps the therapist can be regarded as the spokesperson for the unitary consciousness shared by the patient and therapist. Thus, the therapist's turning his or her attention to either person's subjectivity does not constitute neglect of the other, since the unified concept implies continuing presence and importance of the sector that is not momentarily in focus.

The therapist's capacity for a holistic consciousness may be considered a variant of Winnicott's holding environment. The therapist perceives the patient and himself as a psychological unit. The ability to achieve this perception arises from a precognitive capacity to appreciate subjectively the trans-subjective unity, which in turn derives from a relative fluidity of boundaries and from a powerful shared emotional intimacy. This unity and shared experience enhances independence of thought and feeling, rather than diminishing it. Each person symbolically becomes parent to the other in a therapeutic holding environment. In his role as the child, the therapist explores and enlarges his own inner world as it resonates in reasonable—but not perfect—harmony with the patient–mother. It is this self-exploration that is so effectively employed by the therapist as mothering parent in the construction of the deliberate interventions that are called interpretations.

In the traditional holding environment, the child is thinking and feeling widely and fantastically. But the child's expressive capabilities are as yet severely limited. The good enough mother (parent), although deeply involved from her side, may, like the therapist, superficially seem more detached than the child. This semblance of distance is probably a necessary concomitant of the therapist's or mother's responsibility to act as the formal authority and spokesperson for the unit.

It is worth recalling at this point some recommendations of Goldberg and Gedo (1973). They specified five therapeutic modalities for five different subphases of psychological functioning in the patient. These were:

1. Introspection—for difficulties expectable in adult life.

2. Interpretation—for intrapsychic conflicts associated with neuroses.

3. "Optimal disillusionment" (from Kohut)—for archaic self-aggrandizing or idealizing of others.

4. "Unification"—for failure to integrate a set of personal goals.

5. "Pacification"—for traumatic states.

These authors recommend a significantly different kind of intervention by the analyst for each of the different psychological states. Although the authors do not emphasize the subjective aspect of the analyst's participation, I believe that each mode of intervention would derive from a distinct subjective condition in the analyst. Hence, Goldberg and Gedo's recommendations overlap the following description of four types of intersubjective union of patient and therapist, with emphasis on the therapist's subjective experience of the patient's attitudes and behavior.

Continuing the holding environment analogy, the therapist–mother (parent) may, at times, be in a reverie state, like a mother performing some relatively automatic household chore with the nearby patient–child associating freely. Or the therapist may be focusing intently and exclusively on the patient's verbal and nonverbal behavior, with a minimum of conscious self-absorption. Both stances are highly desirable and fluctuating aspects of optimal therapist involvement in the therapeutic encounter. Blatant or subtle signals emanating from the patient (child) will probably be decisive in determining which of these modes characterizes the therapist's involvement at any given moment.

Four types of patient signals can be identified. In the first instance, the patient's behavior is both intense and inviting. The therapist quite spontaneously attends with acuity and sensitivity, developing and playing with hypotheses regarding the meanings of the patient's behavior. Here the therapist is minimally attentive to his or her own inner fantasies and feelings.

A second situation is also a therapeutically happy one. Here the patient is "babbling." The full, focused attention of the therapist is neither desired nor desirable. In this situation, the therapist has relatively greater involvement in his or her own feelings and fantasies. This is a fluent experience for the therapist, who still feels appropriately attuned to the patient. Out of this associative self-absorption the therapist may well develop some additional understanding of the patient's emotional life. The therapist may thus be constructing a useful interpretation.

The third and fourth signal types are resistive. The third type is the negative analogue of the first. Here the patient clearly demands and obtains the therapist's full attention. But the patient is in pain, which he or she feels is a product of the therapy or the result of failure of therapy. Painful experience cries for relief. The therapist knows what is expected but cannot provide the needed response. The situation is obviously analogous to one in which a child is in a temper tantrum or a panic state with a mother who is completely attentive but frantic with futility. Creative associative activity is suspended on both sides. Later, when and if therapeutic tranquility is restored, the painful impasse may be the subject of productive associations by both the patient and the therapist.

The fourth type of signal repels the therapist. The patient may be talkative or laconic, but the verbal behavior builds barriers and generates distance. In this circumstance the therapist, like the quietly troubled but bewildered mother (parent), drifts into his or her own fantasy pattern. The therapist, on reflection, should be able to shake himself or herself out of this reverie state, which usually does not contain illuminating data regarding the patient. The main value of this state is that it informs the therapist that the patient is pushing him or her away, and an effort can then be made to understand the meaning of this distancing.

Those like the serious student who asked about the distribution of associative time by the therapist may find in the description of these four clinical situations at least a rudimentary answer to the question. The usefulness of this classification will inevitably be limited, because unconscious processes are notoriously resistant to systematic ordering.

It is also important to emphasize that the level of relevant fantasy activity in the therapist is not necessarily indicated by the degree to which the therapist directs conscious attention to his or her own inner life. Sometimes the fantasies are only felt unconsciously and employed intuitively by the therapist. At other times the fantasies are too disturbing, so the therapist represses them, and they are unavailable even for intuitive inclusion in the therapeutic process, with impoverishing effect upon the therapy.

The periods of therapist self-consciousness are often conspicuously frequent and intense in the preliminary stage of interpretation development. It is from his or her own fantasies that the therapist proceeds to construct a *fantasy of meaning* about the patient. This self-consciousness of course develops in a context that includes the patient's psychological process, but the therapist's inner experiences invariably comprise more than a response to the patient's input. This sequence of events concludes with an interpretation by the therapist originating in his or her own subjective experience. Some therapists employ the term *projective identification* to describe the intense emotional experiences they go through and understand to be approximations of a corresponding experience in the patient that is unconscious. But this concept, which excludes the therapist's idiosyncratic role, is too reified and limited to provide adequate understanding of these crucial intersubjective events.

Much psychological activity occurs outside awareness. The therapist's relevant fantasies occur continuously during the therapeutic encounter, and much of the time they are unconscious. It is impossible for any therapist to maintain continuous consciousness of these inner phenomena. In general, interpretations that include some element of this therapist self-attentiveness in their construction tend to be truer, as well as more refined and elegant, than interpretations developed without any self-conscious component on the part of the therapist.

THE ROLE OF PATIENT CRITICISM IN THE DEVELOPMENT OF INTERPRETATION

The therapist should regard as valid every critical sentiment of the patient addressed to the therapist. These may be direct complaints or expressions of resentment. They may also be indirectly expressed by thinly or thickly veiled allusions, by tone of voice and facial expression, or by distrustful questions. Unease in the therapist may suggest undisclosed hostility in the patient. And, of course, the patient's associations can indicate submerged anger to the therapist. The therapist may believe that the degree of validity in the patient's allegation is minuscule relative to the invalid aspect, but even this tiny measure of valid resentment may provide important therapeutic leverage. A heightened sensitivity and an empathic attunement of considerable refinement are required for the therapist to discern the minimal sources of meaning that validate the patient's anger. Otherwise, the often amorphous, fragmented quality of the justifying data will be all too easily dismissable by the defensive therapist.

When a patient complains about the previous therapist, it is useful to assume that the complaint has psychological validity as well as potential pertinence to the current therapist. A middle-aged, married male educator visited me for therapy and remained for several years. Previously, he had been in treatment with another therapist and gained inner confidence from that experience. However, he had terminated that therapy because he felt the therapist had developed a subtly demeaning attitude. He confronted the therapist, who denied such feelings. The patient felt the therapist was not telling the truth. He was angry and hurt; he felt repudiated, and he terminated the relationship. Although he felt that his decision to leave was wise, his understanding of the episode was limited to his awareness that he was insecure, and that he strongly needed his therapist to provide an attitude of unqualified acceptance due to his neurotic hypersensitivity.

He gradually developed a deep sense of security with me, although at the outset he was so fearful that he disguised his therapeutic need of me by telling me that he was coming for consultation about his work rather than for therapy. His fearfulness persisted throughout several years of productive treatment in the form of a major resistance characterized by a frazzled quality of speech and behavior. His sentences either ran on tangentially, or would jump abruptly from theme to theme; he would gesticulate frantically—without evident relationship to his remarks.

He was the youngest child of a large, Eastern European immigrant Jewish family. He felt he had been undervalued by his parents and older siblings because he was the youngest. And to both of us, this devaluation seemed to be demonstrated in the fact that in his childhood home he had no room of his own. I had a strong sense that his feelings of acceptance by me could never undo the power of his feelings of being unwanted by me—as by all others who had emotional importance for him. I would sometimes react to his chaotic behavior by inadvertent distancing from him and retreating into personal reverie. At these times I felt a painful bewilderment, a futility about being able to help him.

At one point a new circumstance at his workplace required that we reschedule his therapy, but he failed to appear at his new time. I called him, and he insisted that our appointment time was the following day. He refused to check his appointment book, accusing me of trying to prove him wrong for my own purposes. He said that although his appointment book was in another room, it was inconvenient to search for it. We agreed on our next meeting time and concluded our conversation in that tense state. When he arrived for his session he was still resentful, telling me he was sure that I had tried to prove he had erred in order to charge him for the missed appointment. I had not really been aware of this motive, but as soon as he stated it, I sensed that he might be correct, and I told him so.

I immediately had a wave of memories from childhood dealing with the enormous economic fears that plagued our family throughout that period. I knew that he had accurately perceived a desperate, grasping quality in me. Although his family had not experienced the same kind of economic privation as mine, I assumed that my acute inner eruption of childhood anxiety was probably resonant with counterpart feelings in him. Various memories involving childhood acts of petty theft or lies now returned to me. I interpreted that his anger at me had been evoked by a fear of being devalued and exploited by me as he had been by the older members of his family.

The initial reaction to aggression is invariably defensive. This defensiveness is often subtle and elusive. Paradoxically, an excessively nondefensive response to aggression is in itself defensive. Unvarying equanimity in the face of an attack may reflect a patronizing or indifferent attitude, both of which are defensive and nontherapeutic. A therapist should experience an attack with some inner discomfort and should then explore the inner meaning of the pain. This discovery in the therapist will eventually lead back to some relevant, but not necessarily identical, issue in the patient that the therapist can now broach in an open, caring, but unflinching way. If the therapist feels only that he or she is the recipient of an inappropriate transferential displacement—which is indeed partially true—the therapist's interventions will invariably convey to the patient that a sick–healthy dichotomy is being maintained, and adequate therapeutic utilization of the incident will not be possible.

It is useful for the therapist to consider a patient's attack or criticism from both quantitative and qualitative standpoints. Typically, when criticized, a therapist may feel that it is just another rationalized excuse for releasing aggression against the therapist. Consequently, the therapist may feel justified in disregarding the bit of truth in the patient's account. It would be better in such an instance for the therapist to ask two questions: (1) is there any truth in the patient's charge, and (2) if so, how much truth is there in the patient's charge? In most instances, the therapist's answer would probably be that the accusation contains only a small amount of truth, and that most of the real meaning of the charge lies concealed within the patient, is neurotic, and requires inter-

pretation. It is the reassurance emanating from these judgments that enables the therapist to relax and work with the
valuable, albeit often small, component of truth in the patient's complaint about the therapist.

When the therapist interprets the criticism too quickly
as negative transference, the patient responds with hurt, angry feelings and a sense of being derided. The patient's hurt
and anger are, in this case, accurate measures of the therapist's
self-serving moves to avoid narcissistic injury. On the other
hand, if the therapist first takes in the criticism and subjects
it to some self-analysis, important benefits can accrue to the
therapeutic situation. First, the patient discovers that angry,
discontented, complaining feelings do not lead to an immediate rejoinder by the therapist, thereby creating a climate
of freedom and acceptance. By taking the patient's assertion
seriously, the therapist validates the patient's view and increases the patient's receptiveness to later comments that may
address unwelcome motives or attitudes in the patient.
Often, the self-analysis by the therapist leads to insight that
illuminates the unconscious aspects of the patient's attack.
So when the therapist returns to the unconscious meanings
of the patient's remarks, the intersubjective climate has mel-
lowed, and the patient may even be eager to learn about his
or her own unconscious motives.

Optimally, the therapist should be defensive enough to
feel the sting in the patient's attack, but secure enough to
explore the meaning of the pain, while simultaneously de-
ferring the interpretation of the patient's problem until there
has been sufficient self-study by the therapist. Under these
favorable conditions, the same interpretation, which, given
earlier, would have provoked massive protest and resentment
will be received with interest and even enthusiasm. A therapist who rejects the subjective validity of unpleasant features
of the patient's communications is sequestering a part of his
subjectivity and is inescapably amputating a portion of the
total intersubjective field.

11

RECLAIMING THE THERAPIST'S SUBJECTIVITY

From the beginning, psychoanalytic therapists have sensed the importance of the therapist's subjectivity, employed it regularly, and attempted to understand its theoretical and technical relevance. These efforts, beginning with Freud, evolved in interesting and valuable ways. Until the present, however, it was not possible to treat in comprehensive detail the therapist's subjectivity as a fundamental element of the therapeutic field.

The chapters of this book explain and illustrate in various ways that therapists' fantasies and desires are crucial ingredients, both initiating and sustaining, of the therapeutic process. They are not mainly reactive phenomena, as implied by the term *countertransference*. The therapist's subjectivity is a basic motivational source and structuring influence in the therapeutic process. When the subjective lives of a specific patient and a specific therapist converge in the therapeutic encounter, they establish a special relationship unlike any other. The uniqueness of the particular relationship is

captured in the therapist's interpretations, and these interpretations also epitomize the analyst's psychological involvement. They are the tip of the therapist's subjectivity.

We can now reclaim the therapist's subjectivity in a detailed and comprehensive way that, in turn, illuminates the
intersubjective foundation of therapeutic action. The net effect is an enlarged understanding and enrichment of the interpretive process. The numerous clinical illustrations in this
book show, in human terms, that we can feel in our own
work how our subjective involvement adds power and meaning to our interpretations.

Once we appreciate the importance of our subjectivity
in working as therapists, we will no longer commit the mistake of setting intersubjectivity and interpretation against one
another, regarding them as mutually exclusive. Instead, we
will see that they exist together, interdependently, and that
valid interpretation always arises from an intersubjective matrix.

Assuming that self comprises the distinctive assemblage
of a person's various psychological tendencies and that selves
really exist only in unstable but creative relation to other
selves, the process of interpretation plays a fundamental role
in the continuous creation of the self of the other. The interpretation registers both the self of the patient and the self of
the giver. The incorporation of the interpretation produces
creative change in the receiving self and provides new self
meaning to the other.

No violence comes to the well-established methods of
psychoanalytic psychotherapy when therapists heed the intersubjective process in doing their work. Indeed, such attention deepens our understanding of therapeutic action.
Although traditional Freudian beliefs about the intrapsychic
origin of neurosis and the intrapsychic nature of cure have
delayed the full integration of the intersubjective dimension,
such an accommodation is now occurring, with beneficial
effects.

The various schools of psychoanalytic thought have each, in differing ways, fostered as well as retarded appreciation of intersubjectivity.

The interpersonal–culturalist school has always emphasized the interrelationship of individual, family, and community. This field theory approach meant that although psychoanalytic treatment focuses on the patient, the patient is seen as functioning in a field of action from which he is inseparable. An explicitly intersubjective point of view is facilitated by such a perspective. At times, however, it has seemed that the interpersonal orientation has been unduly centered on societal influences, with a relative devaluing of the patient's interior life. If such a deemphasis occurs, an authentic intersubjective approach is not being maintained, despite the theoretical congeniality of the intersubjective and the interpersonal. Unconscious resistance to psychological truth can induce a practitioner to overemphasize social and cultural factors in a person's life, when attention should be directed to the individual's inner world.

Kohut's (1977) work on the origins of neurotic traits emphasizes the good or poor quality of parental attunement to the child's needs as the child's personality unfolds. This developmental approach is compatible with the intersubjective premises of this volume. Similarly, self psychologists give great importance to the analyst's attunement, to his vicarious introspection, and to his experience-nearness. These elements of the analyst's involvement sensitize him to his own subjective contribution to the analytic process. Conversely, self psychologists insist that the analyst functions solely as a self-object, possibly entailing neglect of the analyst's total involvement as a person. Specifically, they say, the analyst as self-object should interpret only issues concerning the patient–analyst attunement, since other interpretations may interfere with the patient's self-organizing activity. This limitation of interpretive freedom is not consistent with an intersubjective approach to interpretation.

Freudian psychoanalysis has its own contradictions regarding intersubjectivity. The instinctual orientation of Freud, as already noted, diverts attention from intersubjective considerations. Although the theory of instincts possesses less force in the thinking of today's psychoanalysts than in the past, it maintains some influence on our thinking about the dynamic origin of psychological problems and the process of their cure, that is, the interior origin of conflict and the intrapsychic process of cure. An undue emphasis on interiority in the origin and cure of neurosis entails an obligatory disregard for the role of the therapist's subjectivity.

Yet paradoxically, instinct theory may support the intersubjective process in the following way. Instincts imply drive, that is, motivation. While the working analyst is admonished to eliminate this aspect of his working involvement and to be nontendentious, we know that such a requirement cannot be met. Hence, the analyst always brings wishes and fantasies to an analysis, despite his all too frequent nonacknowledgment of this fact. In this way, the conceptual basis for an intersubjective process is inadvertently established by the theory of drives.

There is another curious contradiction. Freudian analysts suffer a reputation of being excessively wedded to a rigid, outmoded theory. Yet Freudians today maintain an open, ambiguous, and flexible stance vis-à-vis the possibilities of an unfolding therapeutic relationship and are moving ever closer to the intersubjective position presented in this book. Ironically, Freudians have held that their techniques derive from value-neutral attitudes and that this ostensible neutrality has permitted the rich elaboration of fantasy experienced by patients in analysis. The neutrality of psychoanalysts, however, is more apparent than real. In fact, there is a continuous subtextual communication of fantasies and attitudes from analyst to patient. The interplay of these colliding and coalescing sets of fantasies from both patient and therapist initiates and maintains the therapeutic process. Without the silent and often unrecognized fantasy input from the analyst, the patient's sharing of fantasies and feelings would soon stop. The vaunted objectivity of analysts must actually be understood as necessarily subjective in essence.

A focus on the unfolding of intersubjective phenomena in psychoanalytic therapy can contribute to a constructive maturation of our concepts in two ways. In the first place, our psychoanalytic developmental concepts become more congruent with the historical facts, which increasingly show that the individual child develops in an intersubjective relation to parents and family. Second, our well-established treatment methods will be enriched by a much more detailed appreciation of the interplay of fantasies in therapy. The net effect will be a firm grounding of interpretations in both the intersubjective history of the patient and the intersubjective realities of the current therapeutic relationship.

The mainstream of psychoanalysis has accommodated various new theoretical views, sometimes promptly and enthusiastically, at other times belatedly and reluctantly. This expansion includes the contributions of earlier pioneers such as Jung, Rank, and Adler, as well as later thinkers including Ferenczi, Horney, Klein, the various object relationists, and more recently Kohut.

Perhaps a recognition among therapists of all persuasions that they share a common base will help resolve or reduce unnecssary theoretical conflict. The elucidation of the fundamental importance of intersubjective processes in psychoanalysis, whether Freudian, Kohutian, interpersonal, or other, may provide a bridge for better communication and understanding among the various analytic schools.

The study of the intersubjective in psychoanalysis provides three major benefits: First, therapists achieve a continuous self-monitoring function, which becomes recognized by the therapist as an essential element in his psychotherapeutic involvement. This self-consciousness addresses the therapist's ongoing psychological experience as both an originating and reacting phenomenon. Second, the futile and simplistic search for a neat, linear understanding of the therapeutic process can be set aside. Instead, therapists can enjoy a richer sense of the reciprocal contributions to the therapeutic situation, with an increased appreciation of the endless complexities of important therapeutic events. Third, the enriched consciousness of the basic fantasy interplay of patient and therapist enables the analyst to enlarge his database for constructing interpretations and establishes a very useful mediating ambience for the effective conveyance of interpretations.

A full and accurate appreciation of the intersubjective approach also contributes to solving the perennial psychotherapeutic conundrum: How can therapists of various schools claim that they are doing something very different, yet obtaining very similar results? Perhaps the processes are basically the same.

For me, adherence to intersubjective principles has led straight to the realization that my subjectivity is essential to my psychotherapeutic role. From this I have experienced enormous personal and professional enrichment. The truth about the relevance of our subjectivity has been repressed, and it has therefore manifested itself in numerous displaced and disguised forms. It is now time to explore this vital area and recover the lost territory of therapist subjectivity as a powerful resource for well-being.

References

Alexander, F., and French, T. (1946). *Psychoanalytic Therapy*. New York: Ronald Press.

Altman, J. (1989). Personal communication.

Arlow, J. (1979). The genesis of interpretation. *Journal of the American Psychoanalytic Association* 27:193–206.

Bach, S. (1985). *Narcissistic States and the Therapeutic Process*. New York: Jason Aronson.

Bakhtin, M. (1986). *Speech Genres and Other Late Essays*. Trans. V. W. McGee, ed. C. Emerson and M. Holquist. Austin: University of Texas Press.

Balter, L., Lothane, Z., and Spencer, J. (1980). On the analyzing instrument. *Psychoanalytic Quarterly* 49:474–504.

Bettelheim, B. (1982). *Freud and Man's Soul*. New York: Alfred A. Knopf.

Clarke, K., and Holquist, M. (1984). *Mikhail Bakhtin*. Cambridge, MA: Harvard University Press.

Contat, M. (1975). Sartre at seventy, an interview with Jean-Paul Sartre. *New York Review of Books* 22:10–17.

Epstein, L., and Feiner, A. (1979). *Countertransference: The Therapist's Contribution to the Therapeutic Situation*. New York: Jason Aronson.

Ferenczi, S. (1988). *The Clinical Diary of Sandor Ferenczi*. Trans. J. Dupont. Cambridge, MA: Harvard University Press.

Forster, E. M. (1924). *A Passage to India*. New York: Harcourt, Brace.

Foucault, M. (1984–1985). Dream, imagination, and existence. Trans. F. William, ed. K. Hoeller. *Review of Existential Psychology and Psychiatry* 19:29–78.

Freud, S. (1900). The interpretation of dreams. *Standard Edition* 4/5:1–338, 339–627.

——— (1905). Fragment of an analysis: a case history. *Standard Edition* 7:3–122.

——— (1910a). The future prospects of psychoanalytic therapy. *Standard Edition* 11:139–151.

——— (1910b). Five lectures on psycho-analysis. *Standard Edition* 11:3–55.

——— (1911). The handling of dream-interpretation in psycho-analysis. *Standard Edition* 12:89–96.

——— (1912). Recommendations to physicians practicing psychoanalysis. *Standard Edition* 12:109–120.

——— (1915). The unconscious. *Standard Edition* 14:159–215.

——— (1939). *Moses and Monotheism. Standard Edition* 23:7–137.

Gardner, M. R. (1983). *Self Inquiry*. Boston: Little, Brown.

Gedo, J. E. (1981). *Advances in Clinical Psychoanalysis*. New York: International Universities Press.

Gedo, J. E., and Goldberg, A. (1973). *Models of the Mind*. Chicago: University of Chicago Press.

Gill, M. M. (1982). *Analysis of Transference*. Vol. 1: *Theory and Technique*. Monograph 53, *Psychological Issues*. New York: International Universities Press.

Glover, E. (1931). The therapeutic effect of inexact interpretation: a contribution to the theory of suggestion. *International Journal of Psycho-Analysis* 12:397–411.

Greenson, R. (1965). The working alliance and the transference neurosis. *Psychoanalytic Quarterly* 34:155–181.

Habermas, J. (1981). *The Theory of Communicative Action*, vol. 1. Boston: Beacon Press.

Hartmann, H. (1951). Technical implications of ego psychology. *Psychoanalytic Quarterly* 20:31–43.

Heimann, P. (1950). On countertransference. *International Journal of Psycho-Analysis* 31:81–84.

Hill, R. A. (1988). Personal communication.

Hobson, J. A. (1988). *The Dreaming Brain*. New York: Basic Books.

Isakower, O. (1957–1963). Unpublished minutes of curriculum committee and faculty meetings. New York: New York Psychoanalytic Institute.

Jacobs, T. (1985). The use of the self: the analyst and the analytic instrument in the clinical situation. In *Analysts at Work,* ed. J. Reppen, pp. 43–58. Hillsdale, NJ: Analytic Press.

——— (1989). Countertransference, resistance, and the process of self analysis. Paper presented at the meeting of the International Psychoanalytic Association, Rome, Italy, 1989.

Kohut, H. (1977). *The Restoration of the Self.* New York: International Universities Press.

Kris, E. (1951). Ego psychology and interpretation. *Psychoanalytic Therapy* 32: 15–30.

Lacan, J. (1964). *The Four Fundamental Concepts of Psychoanalysis.* Trans. A. Sheridan. New York: W. W. Norton, 1978.

Leavy, S. (1980). *The Psychoanalytic Dialogue.* New Haven, CT: Yale University Press.

Leites, N. (1971). *The New Ego.* New York: Science House.

Levenson, E. (1983). *The Ambiguity of Change.* New York: Basic Books.

Lichtenstein, H. (1977). *The Dilemma of Human Identity.* New York: Jason Aronson.

Little, M. (1951). Countertransference and the patient's response to it. *International Journal of Psycho-Analysis* 32:32–40.

Loewald, H. (1960). On the therapeutic action of psychoanalysis. *International Journal of Psycho-Analysis* 41:16–33. Reprinted in *Papers on Psychoanalysis,* pp. 221–256, 1980. New Haven, CT: Yale University Press.

Loewenstein, R. (1957). Some thoughts on interpretation in the theory and practice of psychoanalysis. *Psychoanalytic Study of the Child* 12:127–150. New York: International Universities Press.

Malcolm, J. (1987). Reflections: *J'appelle un chat un chat. New Yorker* 63:84.

Malcove, L. (1975). The analytic situation: toward a view of the supervisory situation. *Journal of the Philadelphia Association of Psychoanalysis* 2:1–14.

McCarthy, T. (1981). Translator's introduction. In J. Habermas, *The Theory of Communicative Action,* vol. 1, pp. v–xxxvii. Boston: Beacon Press.

Natterson, J. (1986). Interpretation: clinical application. In *Basic Techniques of Psychodynamic Psychotherapy,* ed. M. Nichols and T. Paolino, pp. 309–330. New York: Gardner Press.

Natterson, J., and Grotjahn, M. (1965). Responsive action in psychotherapy. *American Journal of Psychiatry* 122:140–143.

Natterson, J., and Knudson, A. (1960). Observations concerning fear of death in fatally ill children and their mothers. *Psychosomatic Medicine* 22:456–465.

Newson, J. (1977). An intersubjective approach to the systematic description of mother–infant interaction. In *Studies in Mother–Infant Interaction,* ed. H. R. Schaffer, pp. 47–61. New York: Academic Press.

Peterfreund, E. (1983). *The Process of Psychoanalytic Therapy.* Hillsdale, NJ: Analytic Press.

Pine, F. (1985). *Developmental Theory and Clinical Practice.* New Haven, CT: Yale University Press.

Racker, H. (1968). *Transference and Countertransference.* New York: International Universities Press.

Reich, A. (1973). Empathy and countertransference. In *Psychoanalytic Contributions,* pp. 344–360. New York: International Universities Press.

Reik, T. (1948). *Listening with the Third Ear.* New York: Farrar Straus & Giroux.

Roth, P. (1987). *The Counterlife.* New York: Farrar Straus & Giroux.

Rycroft, C. (1979). *The Innocence of Dreams.* New York: Pantheon Books.

——— (1985). *Psychoanalysis and Beyond.* Chicago: University of Chicago Press.

Sartre, J–P. (1981). *The Family Idiot: Gustave Flaubert,* 1821–1827, vol. 1. Trans. C. Cosman. Chicago: University of Chicago Press.

Schafer, R. (1983). *The Analytic Attitude.* New York: Basic Books.

——— (1985). Wild analysis. *Journal of the American Psychoanalytic Association* 33:275–299.

Shields, M. M. (1978). The child as psychologist: contriving the social world. In *Action, Gesture, and Symbol,* ed. A. Lock, pp. 529–556. New York: Academic Press.

Spence, D. (1987). *The Freudian Metaphor: Toward Paradigm Change in Psychoanalysis.* New York: Norton.

Stern, D. (1985). *The Interpersonal World of the Infant: A View from Psychoanalysis and Developmental Psychology.* New York: Basic Books.

Stolorow, R. D., and Atwood, G. (1979). *Faces in a Cloud: Subjectivity in Personality Theory.* New York: Jason Aronson.

——— (1984). *Structures of Subjectivity: Explorations in Psychoanalytic Phenomenology.* Hillsdale, NJ: Analytic Press.

Stolorow, R. D., Brandchaft, B., and Atwood, G. (1987). *Psychoanalytic Treatment: An Intersubjective Approach.* Hillsdale, NJ: Analytic Press.

Stone, L. (1961). *The Psychoanalytic Situation: An Examination of Its Development and Essential Nature.* New York: International Universities Press.

Strachey, J. (1934). The nature of the therapeutic action of psychoanalysis. *International Journal of Psycho-Analysis* 15:127–159.

Tansey, M., and Burke, W. (1989). *Understanding Countertransference, from Projective Identification to Empathy.* Hillsdale, NJ: Analytic Press.

Trevarthan, C. (1980). The foundations of intersubjectivity: development of interpersonal and cooperative understanding in infants. In *The Social Foundation of Language and Thought: Essays in Honor of Jerome Bruner,* ed. D. R. Olson, pp. 316–342. New York: Norton.

Ulman, R., and Stolorow, R. D. (1985). The transference–countertransference neurosis in psychoanalysis: an intersubjective viewpoint. *Bulletin of the Menninger Clinic* 49:37–51.

Vygotsky, L. S. (1962). *Thought and Language.* Ed. and trans. E. Haufmann and G. Vakar, pp. 11–45. Cambridge, MA: M.I.T. Press.

—— (1966). Development of the higher mental functions. In *Psychological Research in the USSR,* ed. A. N. Leontiev. Moscow: Progress Publisher.

Weiss, J., Sampson, H., and the Mt. Zion Psychotherapy Research Group (1986). *The Psychoanalytic Process: Theory, Clinical Observation, and Empirical Research.* New York: Guilford Press.

Winnicott, D. W. (1958). Hate in the countertransference. In *Through Paediatrics to Psycho-Analysis,* pp. 194–203. New York: Basic Books.

—— (1965). *The Maturational Processes and the Facilitating Environment: Studies in the Theory of Emotional Development.* New York: International Universities Press.

—— (1986). *Home Is Where We Start From.* New York: Norton.

Wittgenstein, L. (1942–1946). *Lectures and Conversations on Aesthetics, Psychology and Religious Belief.* Compiled from notes taken by Yorick Smythies, Rush Rhees, and James Taylor, ed. C. Barrett. Berkeley: University of California Press, 1967.

Zetzel, E. (1956). Current concepts of transference. *International Journal of Psycho-Analysis* 37:369–376.

Index